Unlock the Secrets to Bitcoin and Altcoin Profits for Women!

No Gatekeeping

By Savvy Venture

News Flash

Ladies, Crypto Isn't Just a Boys' Club Anymore

Crypto is no longer a niche playground for tech-savvy men—it's a financial revolution where women are stepping up, taking charge, and redefining the rules of the game. Whether you're looking to grow your wealth, protect your assets, or simply explore new opportunities, cryptocurrency offers a world of possibilities. From Bitcoin to Ethereum to the latest altcoins, there's something for everyone, whether you're a cautious investor or a bold risk-taker.

Big News: Crypto Currency Reserves has been initiated World Wide

The creation of a crypto reserve, signaling a major shift in how traditional institutions view digital assets. While details are still emerging, the reserve is expected to include a mix of established and emerging cryptocurrencies. Here's what we know so far:

1. **Bitcoin (BTC):** The undisputed king of crypto, Bitcoin, is likely to be the cornerstone of the reserve. Its scarcity, security, and store-of-value properties make it a natural choice for long-term holdings.

2. **Ethereum (ETH):** Known for its smart contract capabilities and decentralized applications, Ethereum is a strong contender for inclusion. Its versatility and growing ecosystem make it a key player in the crypto space.

3. **Ripple (XRP):** With its focus on cross-border payments and partnerships with major financial institutions, Ripple could play a role in the reserve's strategy for global transactions.

4. **Litecoin (LTC):** Often referred to as the "silver to Bitcoin's gold," Litecoin offers faster transaction times and lower fees, making it a practical addition.

5. **Emerging Altcoins:** The reserve may also include newer coins with high growth potential, such as Solana (SOL), Cardano (ADA), or Polkadot (DOT), which are gaining traction for their innovative technologies.

This move highlights the growing acceptance of cryptocurrency as a legitimate asset class and underscores its potential to reshape the global financial landscape.

Why This Matters for Women

The inclusion of crypto in mainstream financial strategies is a game-changer for women. It's a chance to:

-Take Control: Crypto puts financial power directly in your hands, free from traditional banking systems.

- Diversify Your Portfolio: Adding crypto to your investments can provide a hedge against inflation and economic uncertainty.

- Be Part of the Future: The crypto revolution is just beginning, and women have a unique opportunity to lead the way.

Buckle Up and Dive In!

By the end of this ebook, you'll not only understand the basics of cryptocurrency but also see why it's one of the most exciting opportunities of our time. Whether you're curious about Bitcoin, intrigued by Ethereum, or excited about the latest altcoins, this is your chance to unlock the secrets of the digital revolution.

So, grab your metaphorical helmet and get ready to explore this financial playground where the rules are being rewritten, and the possibilities are endless. Let's dive in together and discover how crypto can empower you to take control of your family financial future! 🚀✨

The Top 20 Cryptocurrency Terms

1. **Bitcoin (BTC):** The first and most well-known cryptocurrency, created in 2009. Often referred to as digital gold.

2. **Blockchain:** A decentralized digital ledger that records all transactions across a network of computers. Think of it as a public database that everyone can see and verify.

3. **Altcoin:** Any cryptocurrency other than Bitcoin. Examples include Ethereum, Litecoin, and Ripple.

4. **Wallet:** A digital tool used to store, send, and receive cryptocurrencies. It can be software (an app on your phone or computer) or hardware (a physical device).

5. **Mining:** The process of verifying transactions on a blockchain and adding them to the ledger. Miners use powerful computers to solve complex math problems to earn new coins.

6. **Token:** A digital asset created on an existing blockchain. Tokens can represent various things, including access to a service or a stake in a project.

7. **Smart Contract:** Self-executing contracts with the terms of the agreement directly written into code. They automatically perform actions when certain conditions are met.

8. **Decentralized Finance (DeFi):** A movement that uses blockchain technology to recreate traditional financial systems (like lending and trading) without intermediaries like banks.

9. **Cryptography:** The practice of securing information using codes, ensuring that only authorized parties can access or tamper with data.

10. **Exchange:** A platform where you can buy, sell, or trade cryptocurrencies for other digital assets or fiat money (like USD). Examples include Coinbase and Binance.

11. **ICO (Initial Coin Offering):** A fundraising method used by new cryptocurrencies to raise capital. Investors buy tokens during the ICO, hoping they will increase in value later.

12. **Fork:** A change or upgrade to a blockchain that creates a split, resulting in a new version of the cryptocurrency. There are hard forks (which create a new coin) and soft forks (which don't).

13. **HODL:** A misspelling of "hold," this term means to keep and not sell your cryptocurrencies, especially during market downturns.

14. **FOMO (Fear of Missing Out):** The anxiety that others are making money in crypto, leading you to invest impulsively.

15. **FUD (Fear, Uncertainty, Doubt):** Negative information or rumors spread intentionally to create fear and confusion about cryptocurrencies, affecting market behavior.

16. **Liquidity:** How easily you can buy or sell an asset without affecting its price. High liquidity means you can quickly convert your crypto into cash or another asset.

17. **Gas Fees:** The fees paid to miners for processing transactions on Ethereum and other blockchains; they compensate miners for their work.

18. **Peer-to-Peer (P2P):** Direct transactions between users without intermediaries, allowing individuals to trade cryptocurrencies directly with one another.

19. **Stablecoin:** A type of cryptocurrency designed to maintain a stable value by being pegged to a reserve asset, like the US dollar. Examples include USDC and Tether (USDT).

20. **Market Cap:** The total value of a cryptocurrency calculated by multiplying the current price by the total circulating supply. It helps gauge the size and importance of a cryptocurrency in the market.

Conclusion

These terms form the foundation of understanding cryptocurrency and its ecosystem. Familiarizing yourself with these concepts will help you navigate the world of crypto more effectively!

Table of Contents

Introduction

What Is Bitcoin and Cryptocurrency?

In this guide, you will learn all about Bitcoin (BTC) and cryptocurrency, how they work, why they exist, and what kind of technology is behind Bitcoin. It wasn't too long ago when people started hearing the words 'Bitcoin' and 'cryptocurrencies.'

Few people outside of the crypto communities knew what they were, and many thought it was just another fad that was bound to fail in a few years or so. The value of one bitcoin was just a few cents then, so obviously, it wasn't worth a lot. For this reason, it was ignored by the masses. There were far more profitable investments one could make, after all.

Those who invested sums of money in the new digital currency either believed in the system proposed by its founder, Satoshi Nakamoto, or they simply wanted to see how it works.

Either way, those who believed were rewarded greatly, and continue to be rewarded, as a single bitcoin now costs thousands of dollars.

It only took Bitcoin five years to breach the $1,000 mark in late 2013, and just a few years later, Bitcoin prices are at an all-time high – way past the $85,000 mark for a single bitcoin!

With skyrocketing prices and extremely fast growth, more and more people are curious about bitcoins and cryptocurrencies.

A Look At Cryptocurrency and Bitcoin's Colorful Past

Imagine money, but without the banks, the paperwork, or the awkward small talk with tellers. That's cryptocurrency! It's digital cash** that lives on the internet, secured by cryptography (fancy math that makes it nearly impossible to counterfeit or double-spend). Unlike the dollars in your wallet, cryptocurrencies operate on decentralized networks powered by blockchain technology.

What's a Blockchain?

Imagine a blockchain as a digital notebook that's copied and shared across many computers. Every time a transaction happens; it's written down in a "block." These blocks are connected in a line, forming a "chain" (that's why it's called a blockchain). It's like a public list that everyone can check, but no one can change or cheat. Because it's so open and secure, you don't need banks or middlemen to manage your money—just you, your cryptocurrency, and the blockchain.

Why Should You Care?

Cryptocurrency isn't just about buying pizza with Bitcoin (yes, that actually happened in 2010). It's a revolution in how we think about money. The first cryptocurrency, Bitcoin, was born in 2009 as a rebel response to the global financial crisis. Its creator, the mysterious Satoshi Nakamoto, wanted to give power back to the people, no banks, no governments, just pure peer-to-peer transactions.

Since then, the crypto world has exploded with thousands of digital coins, each with its own superpower. Some, like Bitcoin, are the gold standard of crypto—scarce, secure, and perfect for storing value. Others, like Ethereum, let you run smart contracts and build decentralized apps (think of it as the app store of the blockchain world). And then there are the privacy coins, the meme coins, and everything in between.

Why This Matters for Women

Women, the world of cryptocurrency isn't just for men anymore—it's a space where you can explore new ways to build wealth, protect your money, and take charge of your financial future. Whether you're someone who plays it safe or loves taking risks, there's a cryptocurrency out there that fits your needs. Now's your chance to get involved and help shape the future of finance! 💪✨

Cryptocurrencies are digital currencies which are electronic in nature. They do not have a physical form like paper money or coins which you probably have in your wallet right now. You can't hold them physically, but you can buy things with them.

Depending on the merchant you're doing business with, they may accept more than one cryptocurrency as payment.

According to CoinMarketCap (https://coinmarketcap.com), there are more than 1,000 active cryptocurrencies right now. If you're looking to invest your hard-earned cash but can't afford Bitcoin prices right now, there are plenty of alternative cryptocurrencies to choose from, such as Ethereum, Litecoin, Ripple, Dash, Monero, Zcash, and more.

We would, of course, advise you to do some in-depth research on the cryptocurrency you want to invest in, as not all cryptocurrencies are equal. Some are more stable than others and would, therefore, make for better investments.

Bitcoin is not the world's first cryptocurrency, but it is the most successful. Many have come before it, but all have failed. And the reason for failure? Virtual currency had an inherent problem – it was easy to double-spend. You could pay $100 to one merchant and use the same amount of money to pay for a second merchant! Scammers and fraudsters simply loved this loophole.

Fortunately, in 2007, Satoshi Nakamoto started working on the Bitcoin concept. On October 31st the following year, he released his white paper entitled "Bitcoin: A Peer-to-Peer Electronic Cash System", which outlined a payment system that addressed the double-spending problem of digital currencies.

It was a brilliant concept that drew the attention of the cryptographic community. The Bitcoin Project software was registered in SourceForge just a little over a week after the white paper was published.

In January 2009, the first-ever Bitcoin block, called the 'Genesis Block,' was mined. Days later, block 170 recorded the first-ever bitcoin transaction between Hal Finney and Satoshi Nakamoto.

The very next year, in November 2010, Bitcoin's market cap exceeded $1,000,000! This was a very pivotal moment in the development of Bitcoin, as this led to more people getting interested and investing in Bitcoins. The price at this point was $0.50/BTC.

However, in June 2011, Bitcoin experienced the so-called "Great Bubble of 2011" after reaching an all-time high of $31.91/BTC. Just four days after reaching its highest price, the exchange rate plummeted to just $10/BTC.

A Lesson in Patience: Why Holding Pays Off

Many investors panicked during Bitcoin's steep drops in recent years, selling at a loss out of fear. For example, during the 2022 crypto winter, Bitcoin plummeted from its all-time high of nearly $69,000 to below $16,000, causing widespread panic. Those who sold during this period locked in their losses, while those who held on saw the market recover.

Fast forward to 2024, and Bitcoin has not only bounced back but has shattered expectations, reaching new all-time highs above $113,000. This recovery was fueled by factors like the approval of Bitcoin ETFs, institutional adoption, and the 2024 Bitcoin halving, which reduced supply and increased demand.

The lesson? Patience pays off. Those who kept their Bitcoin during the tough times were rewarded as the price soared beyond everyone's wildest dreams. This pattern isn't unique to Bitcoin—it's a reminder that crypto markets are volatile, but holding through the dips can lead to incredible gains.

Current Events in Crypto (2025)

1. Bitcoin ETFs Driving Demand: The approval of Bitcoin ETFs by the SEC has brought a flood of institutional money into the market, pushing prices to new highs.

2. Ethereum's Upgrades: Ethereum's transition to proof-of-stake and ongoing scalability improvements have solidified its position as the leading platform for decentralized applications.

3. Altcoin Season: Coins like Solana (SOL), Avalanche (AVAX), and Chainlink (LINK) are gaining traction, offering high-growth opportunities for risk-tolerant investors.

4. Regulatory Developments: Governments worldwide are working on clearer crypto regulations, which could further legitimize the industry and attract more investors.

Fidelity Predicts: $1B per 1 BTC by 2038 — 2040

Jurrien Timmer, Director of Global Macro at Fidelity Investments, predicts a staggering future for Bitcoin, suggesting that the value of a single Bitcoin could soar to $1 billion by 2038 to 2040.

Timmer's demand model is rooted in Metcalfe's Law. It claims the value of Bitcoin will grow steadily to **about $1 million per full Bitcoin by 2030**. A network like Bitcoin comprises a set of nodes that form connections with one another and follow a protocol, a group of rules.

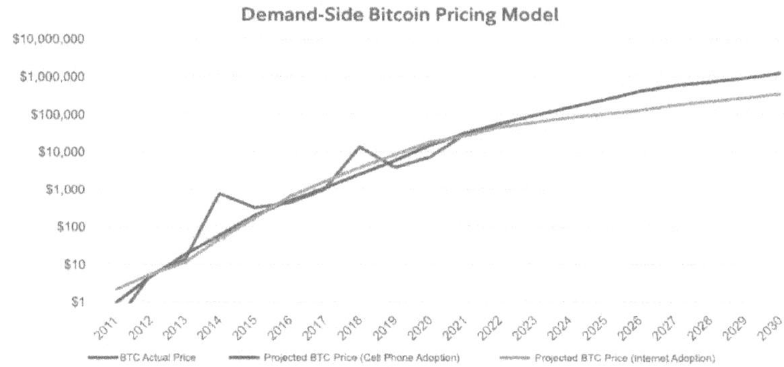

	2022	2023	2024	2025	2030
Cell Phone Adoption	$55,845	$91,757	$149,244	$239,578	$1,246,088
Internet Adoption	$44,436	$60,070	$80,489	$100,229	$343,186

Data Source: World Bank Economic Data & Coin Metrics, 05/31/2022.

Why This Matters for You

Whether you're a seasoned investor or just starting out, the crypto market offers unparalleled opportunities—but it requires a strong stomach and a long-term mindset. By staying informed and avoiding emotional decisions, you can position yourself to ride the waves of volatility and come out on top.

So, the next time the market dips, remember: Hold on tight and add more to your bags. The best might be yet to come. 🚀✨

What's interesting about Bitcoin is that while all transactions are public and nothing is hidden from anyone, no one actually knows anything about Satoshi Nakamoto. Many have speculated that he is not just one person but rather a collective pseudonym for a group of cryptographic developers. Some have come forward claiming to be Satoshi, but to date, his real identity remains a secret.

Why Do Cryptocurrencies Exist?

Many people have started thinking that cryptocurrencies, Bitcoin in particular, are on the brink of replacing our national currencies such as the US Dollar, British Pound Sterling, Euro, Canadian Dollar, and more. This is because cryptocurrencies have started to become very viable alternatives to traditional currency.

Cryptocurrencies exist to address weaknesses in traditional currencies, which are, of course, backed by central banks and governments. This makes traditional currencies prone to corruption and manipulation, among a host of other issues.

Unlike traditional currencies, there is no governing body that backs Bitcoin and other cryptocurrencies, which means they aren't subjected to anybody's whims.

Bitcoin is completely decentralized, open-source, and transparent. This means that you can see all the transactions that have ever been done on the network, and you can check and review the blockchain data yourself to verify the authenticity of each transaction.

Bitcoin runs on highly complex mathematical algorithms to regulate the creation of new bitcoins and to make sure no double spending ever occurs on the network (remember, this is the Achilles' heel of failed virtual currencies before Bitcoin).

The Bitcoin code is so secure and advanced that it's virtually impossible to cheat the system, so if you're thinking you can create an unlimited number of bitcoins, you're greatly mistaken.

One of the main problems of traditional currency is that these aren't limited in number. This means that governments and central banks can print more money when they see fit.

When more money is printed and enters the economy, this reduces the purchasing power of our paper money, which means we need to spend more on an item we've only spent a few dollars on before; this is called inflation.

Bitcoin, on the other hand, is a different story. The Bitcoin Protocol states that only 21,000,000 bitcoins can ever be mined and created, which means that bitcoin is, in fact, a scarce resource.

Also, like national currencies, bitcoins are divisible, much like cents to a dollar. The smallest bitcoin unit is called a Satoshi, and it is 1/100,000,000 of a bitcoin. This means you can invest a few thousand Satoshis at a time until you finally get a whole bitcoin.

Of course, if you go this route, it may take you some time to get to 1 BTC, but if the price continues to skyrocket, then buying a few Satoshis regularly may pay off in the long term.

Another reason why cryptocurrencies are gaining in popularity is that they are highly portable, meaning you can bring them with you anywhere you go. You can do the same with physical money and gold. However, a large amount will lead to a heavy load on your wallet or bag.

Try putting a million dollars in a briefcase or carrying a bag of gold! It's certainly not as light as it looks in movies.

With cryptocurrency, you have different wallet choices, all of which are highly portable, so you can easily make payments whenever and wherever you want.

Bitcoins are not subject to bank and government regulations. This means you don't need to pay those hefty bank fees which you incur whenever you send payments to other people.

You also don't need to wait several hours or maybe even a few days for your payments to clear or post, as Bitcoin payments are made almost instantly (usually in 10-45 minutes).

Understanding Bitcoin

How Bitcoin Works

In this section, we will do our best to explain the Bitcoin process as simply as possible without going into too much technical jargon.

The first thing you need to do is get yourself some bitcoins. You can either mine them yourself, receive some as payment for goods or services, or buy them at a Bitcoin exchange like Coinbase or Kraken. There are different wallets for you to store your new bitcoins in.

You can use a desktop wallet, mobile app wallet, paper wallet, hardware wallet, or an online wallet. There are pros and cons to each type of wallet. However, most experts agree that online wallets, specifically those on exchange sites, are not so secure because both your private and public keys are saved online. This makes your wallet highly vulnerable to hackers.

When you've selected the most suitable wallet for your needs, you can then start making Bitcoin transactions. To send Bitcoin to another user, all you have to do is get their email or Bitcoin address, enter the amount you wish to send, write a quick note to tell them what the payment is for (this is optional), and hit the Send button!

Alternatively, if you've got the QR code to their Bitcoin wallet, you can simply scan it and hit Send. The transaction will appear in the other person's account in a short period of time, usually between 10-45 minutes. The reason for this 'wait' is explained more fully in the next section.

And that's it! Bitcoin transactions are quick, safe, cheap, and the perfect alternative to paying with bank-issued credit and debit cards, and even paying in cash.

The Technology Behind Bitcoin

On the surface, Bitcoin transactions appear to be fast and easy – and they truly are. However, behind the scenes, the technology that makes the Bitcoin network run seamlessly is a massive ledger known as the blockchain.

It's massive because it contains a record of all Bitcoin transactions that have ever taken place since Bitcoin was first released in 2009.

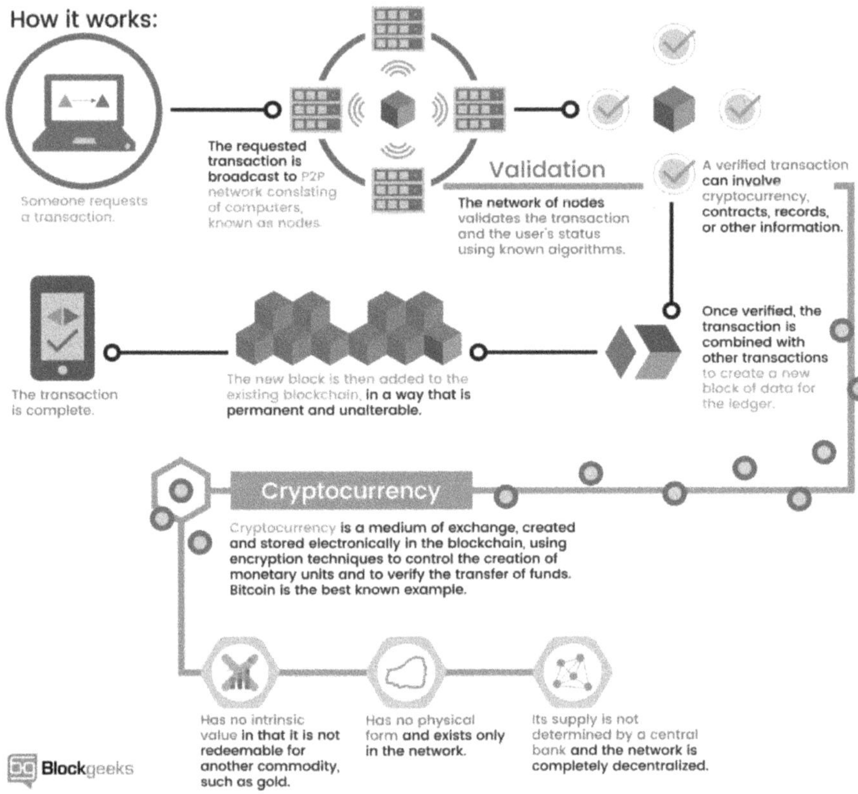

As more time passes by and more transactions occur, the size of the blockchain will continue to grow. So here is how the blockchain works:

(Image Source: BlockGeeks.com)

When you send a payment, your wallet or app sends out a request to the entire Bitcoin network, which is made up of computers or nodes. These nodes then validate your transaction using known algorithms.

Once your transaction is verified and confirmed, it is then combined with other transactions to create a new block of data for the blockchain.

This new block is then added to the end of the blockchain. When this happens, the transaction becomes complete and is now permanent.

This entire process takes about 10-45 minutes from start to finish (this is why Bitcoin transactions don't happen instantly). Once the transaction is finalized, no one can undo or delete the transaction. The person you've sent the Bitcoin payment to (the receiver) will now see your payment in their wallet.

So, who verifies and confirms transactions if there's no central body governing the network?

The answer is the miners. The miners are literally the lifeblood of the entire Bitcoin network. Some have even compared miners to hamsters in the wheel that keep the entire Bitcoin network going! And this is true.

What is Bicoin Mining?

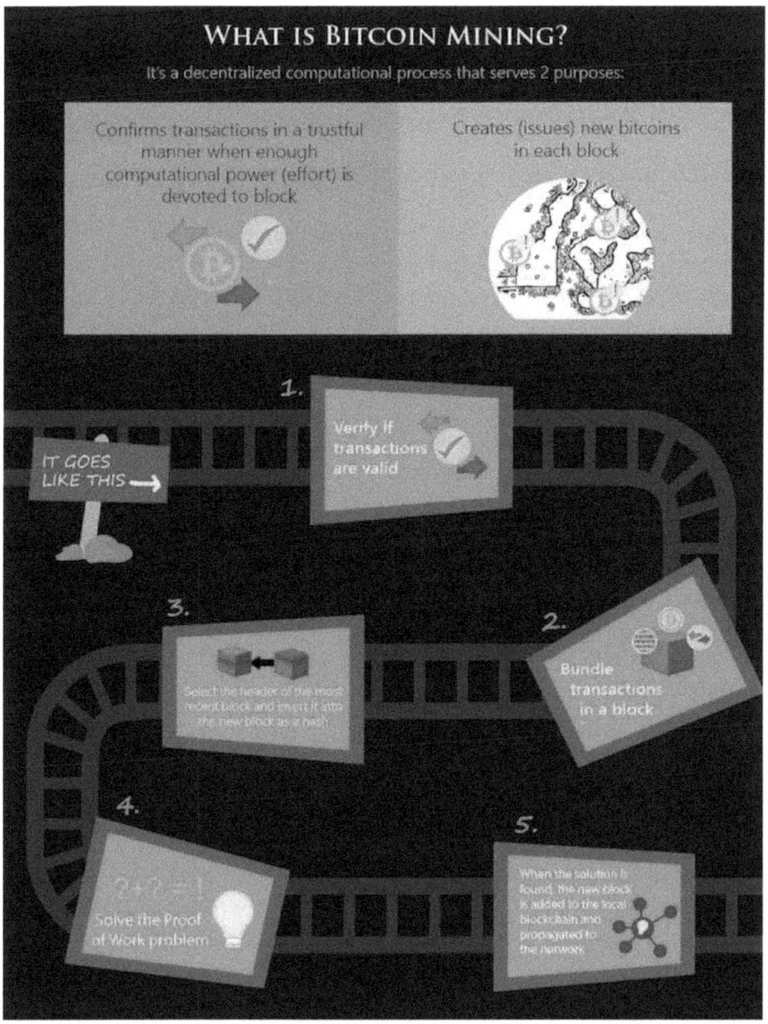

Miners play such a huge role in the success of Bitcoin that they truly deserve getting rewarded in precious bitcoins. Without them, no new blocks would be created and added to the blockchain.

If nothing is added to the blockchain, no transactions are ever finalized. This means no Bitcoin payments are sent and received by anyone on the network. No new bitcoins will be created.

Because miners are indispensable to the Bitcoin network, they are compensated for their hard work in terms of bitcoins (it would not make any sense to reward them in traditional paper currency). They are almost like employees on the network.

Since there are only a limited number of bitcoins (21 million), the number of bitcoins that miners are paid with will continue to dwindle until all bitcoins are exhausted by around 2140.

The Role Of Mining In The Creation Of New Bitcoins

You can own bitcoins using a few methods. The easiest way is to buy some bitcoins on a Bitcoin exchange platform, though, of course, Bitcoin prices are so high now that you'll need to make a sizeable investment.

The other method is not to use any money and instead simply mine bitcoins using computer hardware.

It's important to note here that the main and integral purpose of mining is the creation or release of new bitcoins, which can then be available on the network.

As of October 2023, approximately 19.5 million bitcoins have been mined, leaving around 1.5 million bitcoins left to be mined. This means roughly 93% of Bitcoin's total supply of 21 million coins is already in circulation.

Current Mining Status

- As of now, approximately 19 million Bitcoins have already been mined.

How Mining Works

- Bitcoin has a built-in halving event that occurs approximately every four years (every 210,000 blocks mined). During a halving, the block reward that miners receive for adding new blocks to the blockchain is halved. Initially, the reward was 50 bitcoins per block, but it has decreased over time:

- 2009: 50 BTC

- 2012: 25 BTC (First halving)
- 2016: 12.5 BTC (Second halving)
- 2020: 6.25 BTC (Third halving)
- 2024: 3.125 BTC (Fourth halving)

Remaining Bitcoins to be Mined by 2140

- The final Bitcoin is expected to be mined around the year 2140. At this point, the mining reward will have diminished significantly due to the halving events.

- The process of mining new Bitcoins will slow down over time, and by the year 2140, it is estimated that nearly all 21 million Bitcoins will have been mined, with close to 0.000001 BTC left to be mined as the block reward approaches zero.

Conclusion

By 2140, virtually all Bitcoins will have been mined, with only a tiny fraction remaining due to the mining mechanism and halving schedule. This scarcity is one of the fundamental aspects of Bitcoin's value proposition in the cryptocurrency market and the lucrative possibilities to get in now.

That fewer and fewer bitcoins can be mined as time goes by drives up the interest of the people in the currency, because rarity is desirable and highly marketable.

This increases the value of Bitcoin because it operates using a network— the larger the network, the greater use you can get out of Bitcoin.

Key Points About Bitcoin's Supply

1. Scarcity: With only 1.5 million Bitcoins left, the supply is becoming increasingly scarce, which is a key factor driving Bitcoin's value.

2. Halving Events: Every four years, the block reward for miners is cut in half. The next halving happened in 2024, reducing the reward from 6.25 BTC to 3.125 BTC per block.

3. Final Bitcoin: The last Bitcoin is projected to be mined around the year 2140, after which no new Bitcoins will enter circulation.

Why This Matters

- Investment Potential: As Bitcoin becomes scarcer, its value is likely to increase, especially with growing adoption and demand.

- Mining Dynamics: Miners will increasingly rely on transaction fees rather than block rewards as the supply of new Bitcoins dwindles.

- Long-Term Strategy: For investors, understanding Bitcoin's supply dynamics is crucial for making informed decisions.

If you'd like real-time updates on the number of Bitcoins mined, you can check blockchain explorers like [Blockchain.com] (https://www.blockchain.com/explorer) or [Bitcoin.com](https://explorer.bitcoin.com/btc). 🚀✨

Bitcoin Mining Resources

- If you're interested in Bitcoin mining, there are various resources available to help you understand the process, set up your mining operation, and stay informed about the latest developments in the field. Here's a comprehensive list of resources:

- 1. Educational Resources

  - Bitcoin.org: The official Bitcoin website offers an extensive section on mining, including guides and FAQs.

  - Bitcoin Mining Overview (https://bitcoin.org/en/how-to-mine-bitcoin)

  https://www.investopedia.com/terms/b/bitcoihttps://www.investopedia.com/terms/b/bitcoin-mining.asp)

  https://www.bitmain.com/)https://www.bitmain.com/)

  https://www.microbt.com/)https://www.microbt.com/)

  https://github.com/ckolivahttps://github.com/ckolivas/cgminer)

  https://github.com/luke-jr/bfgminerhttps://github.com/luke-jr/bfgminer)

  https://easyminer.net/)https://easyminer.net/)

  https://slushpool.com/)https://slushpool.com/)

  https://www.f2pool.com/)https://www.f2pool.com/)

  https://antpool.com/)https://antpool.com/)

https://whattomine.com/)https://whattomine.com/)

htthttps://www.cryptocompare.com/mining/calculator/)

https://bitcointalk.org/)https://bitcointalk.org/)

https://www.reddit.cohttps://www.reddit.com/r/BitcoinMining/)

https://www.coindesk.com/)https://www.coindesk.com/)

https://www.theblock.co/)https://www.theblock.co/)

Also, be on the lookout for credit card offers that provide crypto coins in exchange for points, such as travel or dining experiences.

Now that you know what Bitcoin and cryptocurrency are all about, let's move to the next guide, where you will learn how the value of Bitcoin is determined.

Bitcoin Value – How Is The Value Of Bitcoin Determined

Bitcoin has been getting a huge amount of hype recently. It's one of the many digital currencies in existence today that acts and functions like regular money but exists entirely electronically—like data inside computers.

And that can be kind of confusing because if there is no actual physical Bitcoin:

How can it have value?

- How can you use digital currency in a physical world?
- Well, actually, the question of how Bitcoin has any value at all isn't so far off from the question of how most real-world money has value.

First off, Bitcoin has no actual intrinsic value, which means that it has little to no use to us outside of its economic context. But the same can be said for most real-world currencies: money only has value because the government that issues it says it does.

This is called 'fiat currency' because its value is not tied to any physical commodity and relies on the backing of a government.

But unlike fiat currency, Bitcoin does not have an issuing authority that gives it value. Bitcoin is a decentralized currency, meaning there is no governing body that regulates its production and transactions.

It doesn't answer to any government or organization, so there isn't really a reason why it should have value, yet it does—and it can all be boiled down to utility, scarcity, and supply and demand.

Bitcoin's Value Comes from Its Usefulness

To understand why Bitcoin is valuable, let's start with the basics of how it works. Bitcoin operates on a computer network where users are connected, and all transactions are recorded in a digital ledger called a blockchain. Think of the blockchain as a chain of blocks, where each block contains a list of transactions.

The people who maintain this ledger are called miners. They work hard to verify transactions and add them to the blockchain, similar to how gold miners dig for gold. In return, they are rewarded with Bitcoin. Just like gold, Bitcoin is limited in supply—only 21 million will ever exist.

Now, why is Bitcoin valuable? It's because of its utility—its usefulness in three key areas: decentralization, security, and ease of transactions.

1. Decentralization: Bitcoin isn't controlled by any government, bank, or company. Instead, it runs on a peer-to-peer network, meaning users can send and receive Bitcoin directly without a middleman. This makes Bitcoin a truly global, borderless currency. You can send Bitcoin to anyone, anywhere, without worrying about exchange rates or borders.

2. Security: All Bitcoin transactions are recorded on the blockchain, which is public and nearly impossible to tamper with. This makes Bitcoin secure and transparent.

3. Ease of Transactions: Traditional financial systems (like banks, credit cards, or money transfer services) rely on middlemen to process transactions. These middlemen charge fees and can slow things down. Bitcoin cuts out the middleman, allowing you to send money directly to someone else quickly and often at a lower cost.

In short, Bitcoin's value comes from its ability to let people exchange money securely, quickly, and without relying on banks or governments. It's a new way to think about money and finance, giving you more control over your own funds.

This means that no single person or group of people has a hold on the network—which, in turn, means that bitcoins can remain fully transparent and neutral in its transactions.

But if there is no official body acting as a regulator, who can you trust to make sure that transactions do go through? The answer: no one. And it sounds bad, but it's actually a good thing.

The Bitcoin system is designed to operate without the need for trust. See, it's not simply a digital currency—it's a cryptocurrency, which means that it is heavily based on encryption techniques to keep it safe.

Instead of operating based on customer trust, Bitcoin operates using tried and tested mathematics (more on that later). Cheating the network is impossible due to its public environment.

Not only that, but the system is encrypted so that trying to commit fraud would require an extremely large amount of computing power, which would by then have been more useful if you just used it to mine more bitcoins.

The security system, aside from ensuring the reliability of Bitcoin transactions, also ensures that the identity of Bitcoin users can be protected. Unlike with credit cards, your account number does not have any value in your transactions, which are ultimately verified using a private and public key.

It works like this: you put a digital signature on your transactions using your private key, which can be verified by the users of the network using your public key. The keys are encrypted so that the public key can only ever work if you have used the correct private key in the first place.

This means that:

1. Your identity can't be stolen by criminals to make fraudulent transactions in your name.

2. You can choose to remain completely anonymous in the Bitcoin network, which may prove useful for some.

Lastly, bitcoins have the possibility of providing an ease of convenience that surpasses the traditional paying methods that we already have now.

According to the Bitcoin site, using bitcoins allows you "to send and receive bitcoins anywhere in the world at any time. No bank holidays. No borders. No bureaucracy. Bitcoin allows its users to be in full control of their money."

Bitcoins Are Incredibly Scarce

Fiat currency has a technically unlimited supply in the sense that governments can produce money whenever they want. Obviously, they don't do that because it will lead to inflation, so the production and release of money is controlled by the government based on intensive research on market trends and needs. Bitcoin, as you might have guessed, does not work the same.

Because Bitcoin is decentralized, there is no authority that decides when to make new bitcoins. The system is designed so that new bitcoins can only be created as part of a reward system for the miners.

And the reward is well-deserved: the backbone of the Bitcoin system is cryptography, or the art of writing and solving codes, which requires a hefty amount of work to solve.

To update the blockchain, miners from all over the world have to race to solve a specific math problem called SHA-256, which stands for Secure Hash Algorithm 256-bit.

It's basically a math problem wherein you're given an output and you're supposed to find the input, like solving for x and y given that $x + y = 2$.

Miners invest a lot of money in these supercomputers (as well as the huge amount of electricity needed to run them) to mine new bitcoins.

The cap on Bitcoin production is there to ensure that Bitcoin wouldn't ever be hyperinflated.

Supply And Demand Affects Bitcoin Value Directly

The market value of Bitcoin—that is, the money that people are willing to pay for it—follows the same old basic demand and supply rule: a high demand increases its price, and a low demand decreases it.

Before we go any further, just remember that the value of something is not the same as its price; value is what people perceive a product is worth, while price is what they pay for it. Even so, value and price go hand in hand: the price of something is directly related to its value and vice versa.

According to an article in The Economist, the increasing trend in the price of Bitcoin is what drives people to invest in it.

People are investing because they believe that, following the trend so far, they will be able to sell their Bitcoins for a much higher price in the future, which the article argues is a perfect example of the greater fool theory.

Basically, the greater-fool theory states that the price of a product is determined not by its intrinsic value but by the beliefs and expectations that consumers put on the product.

From this perspective, the surging price of Bitcoin serves not to increase its actual value but to render it irrelevant.

The market is driving the price of Bitcoin up because of the growing belief that it will be worth more in the future, not because they think its value is increasing over time. However, some people argue that the surge in Bitcoin prices that the past year has seen is not indicative of it being a bubble.

On the Bitcoin site itself, it argues that it is not a bubble, citing that bubbles are artificially overvalued products that tend to correct themselves eventually.

It cites its relatively small and young market as the reason for the volatility in Bitcoin prices—that "choices based on individual human action by hundreds of thousands of market participants are the cause for Bitcoin's price to fluctuate as the market seeks price discovery."

1. It argues that the volatility of Bitcoin prices is due to many forces such as:
2. Loss of confidence in Bitcoin
3. A large difference between value and price that is not based on the fundamentals of the Bitcoin economy
4. Increased press coverage stimulating speculative demand
5. Fear of uncertainty
6. Old-fashioned irrational exuberance and greed

As such, Bitcoin argues that its growing prices can be attributed to more and more people finding the product increasingly worth their money based on its utility, thereby validating its value.

The approval of Bitcoin (BTC) and Ethereum (ETH) NFTs by regulatory bodies like the Securities and Exchange Commission (SEC) could significantly influence the price and overall market perception of both cryptocurrencies. Here are some potential impacts to consider:

1. Increased Legitimacy and Institutional Adoption

- Regulatory Clarity: SEC approval provides legal recognition and regulatory clarity for NFTs on these blockchains. This can instill confidence among institutional investors who may have been hesitant to enter the market due to regulatory uncertainties.
- Institutional Investment: Increased legitimacy could lead to more institutional money flowing into Bitcoin and Ethereum, potentially driving up their prices as demand rises.

2. Market Expansion and Use Cases

- New Use Cases for Ethereum: Ethereum is already a popular platform for NFTs. SEC approval could further validate Ethereum's role in the NFT space, leading to increased usage and new projects that leverage Ethereum's smart contracts. This could enhance Ethereum's value proposition and drive demand.

- Bitcoin's NFT Market: While Bitcoin is not primarily known for NFTs, if SEC approval leads to innovations allowing Bitcoin-based NFTs, it could diversify Bitcoin's use cases and attract new users and investment, potentially enhancing its price.

3. Investor Sentiment

- Positive Market Sentiment: Approval from the SEC could generate positive media coverage and hype around both cryptocurrencies, attracting retail and institutional investors who may want to capitalize on the NFT trend.

- Fear of Missing Out (FOMO): The excitement surrounding NFTs in the context of Bitcoin and Ethereum could lead to FOMO among investors, driving prices higher as more people look to get involved at the early stages of a potentially growing market segment.

4. Impact on Supply and Demand Dynamics

- Increased Demand for NFTs: If NFTs on Bitcoin and Ethereum gain traction, the demand for these cryptocurrencies may increase as users and collectors require the respective tokens to interact with NFT marketplaces.

- Potential Reduced Selling Pressure: As more people buy and hold BTC and ETH for NFT-related activities, there could be less selling pressure on these assets, potentially stabilizing or increasing their prices.

5. Price Volatility

- Initial Price Spike: The immediate reaction to SEC approval may lead to a price spike due to speculative trading, followed by volatility as the market adjusts and digests the news.

- Long-Term Trends: In the long run, the impact will depend on the sustained adoption of NFTs and broader market trends regarding

Bitcoin and Ethereum, including regulatory developments, technological advancements, and market sentiment.

Overall, SEC approval of Bitcoin and Ethereum NFTs has the potential to positively influence the price of both cryptocurrencies by enhancing legitimacy, attracting institutional interest, and expanding use cases. However, price movements will also depend on broader market conditions, investor sentiment, and the actual adoption of NFTs. As always, investing in cryptocurrencies remains speculative and comes with inherent risks, so it's important to conduct thorough research and consider market trends when making investment decisions.

So, in summary: Bitcoin's utility and scarcity give it value, but its prices seem to send opposing signals as to whether it's truly valuable or not.

With more and more people beginning to show interest in Bitcoin, perhaps we are barely scratching the surface of what its true value may be.

Different Techniques To Acquire Bitcoin

There are many different techniques to acquiring bitcoins, and in this guide, we will show you the most popular methods of getting yourself some units of the world's most popular cryptocurrency.

Buy Some Bitcoins

Buying bitcoins is a very simple and straightforward process. You can simply go to a Bitcoin exchange website such as Coinbase or Kraken and exchange your US Dollars, British Pounds, Euros, Canadian Dollars, and other supported currencies (this will depend on the platform) into some bitcoins.

Of course, with the ever-increasing value of Bitcoin, this is easier said than done.

Right now, you can expect to shell out more than $85,000 for a single Bitcoin! The good news is that you don't have to buy a whole Bitcoin. Each Bitcoin can be divided into 100 million units called Satoshis (named after Bitcoin founder, Satoshi Nakamoto).

This means you can buy a few thousand Satoshis for a few dollars. While this won't make you rich, you can at least get a feel for how bitcoins and cryptocurrency work.

Here are some of the best places where you can buy bitcoins:

Cryptocurrency Exchanges

There are plenty of platforms where you can buy and sell cryptocurrency. The most popular ones that have been around for a few years are Coinbase, Kraken, Gemini, Coinmama, and Binance US.

You'll have to do some research, however, to determine whether your state or country is supported and what currencies and payment methods they accept, as each platform has its own rules and regulations.

The transaction fees involved will also vary on each platform, so you'll definitely have to look around to find the best cryptocurrency exchange that suits your Bitcoin needs.

Cash Exchanges

If you want to avoid Bitcoin exchange platforms and pay directly in cash (or another payment method that's popular in your local area), use cash exchanges like LocalBitcoin or Wall of Coins. These platforms allow you to trade directly with another person.

There are no expensive transaction fees involved. However, they may charge a fee for successful trades. We would suggest that you look for a platform that offers an escrow service to make sure the seller doesn't run away with your hard-earned cash!

Trade Your Other Cryptocurrencies For Bitcoin

If you've got a digital wallet full of other cryptocurrencies, you can easily trade these for bitcoins. You can go to sites like ShapeShift.io, which allows you to quickly trade your non-Bitcoin cryptocurrency for bitcoins.

You don't even need an account to make a trade. Simply enter the amount you wish to convert or trade, your Bitcoin address, and your cryptocurrency refund address. That's it! You'll have your new bitcoins in a few minutes.

Get Paid With Bitcoins

Getting paid with bitcoins is not a complicated process at all. You simply need to have your own Bitcoin wallet so you can start receiving payments.

For starters, you can create a free online wallet on Blockchain.info or Coinbase.

All you need is a valid email address to sign up and begin receiving payments! Once your wallet is set up, you can either generate a QR code or use the long alphanumeric address and send it to the person you wish to receive bitcoins from.

Here are some ideas on how you can get paid with bitcoins:

Work For Bitcoins

There are many different types of work you can do to get paid in Bitcoin. It doesn't matter if you work online or offline, as making and receiving Bitcoin payments is so simple that you don't really need technical know-how to do it.

Solopreneurs find this payment method much more convenient as they don't need to wait 24-48 hours (or more for international workers) to receive bank transfers from their clients. They can receive their payment, salary, or wages in just a few minutes.

It's a big relief to workers knowing they don't need to wait in limbo, unsure if they're going to get paid for their hard work or not. Employers or clients also like the idea of not paying those exorbitant bank fees for transfers, especially to workers or freelancers overseas.

With Bitcoin payments, they get to save plenty of money just in bank fees alone!

Sell Products Or Services

Whether you are an online shop or a brick-and-mortar store, you can choose to receive payments in Bitcoin. With a growing community of Bitcoin users, you're bound to get new and repeat customers who will do business with you simply because you're forward-thinking enough to accept Bitcoin payments.

The added benefit to customers is that they can easily send you payments straight from their Bitcoin wallets while you receive their payments almost instantly. It's really a win-win situation for both you and your customers!

For online shops, you can use plugins or scripts to start accepting Bitcoin payments on your site. If you're unsure of how to do this, it's best to hire a developer to ensure it's set up correctly (you don't want those Bitcoin payments going somewhere else!).

When your customers go to your checkout page, they'll see the Bitcoin option and select if they want to pay using bitcoins.

For local shops like hotels, restaurants, bars, cafes, flower shops, groceries, etc., if you want to receive Bitcoin payments in person, all you have to do is print your wallet's QR code and pin it near your cash register.

When your customers are ready to pay, simply direct them to the QR code, have them scan it on their mobile phones, enter the amount they need to pay, hit Send, and wait for your bitcoins to arrive.

Oh, and don't forget to add a giant 'Bitcoin Accepted Here' sign at the entrance to invite the Bitcoin community to come inside! To attract even more Bitcoin users, add your business to Coinmap and other similar sites where the Bitcoin community hangs out and searches for places where they can spend their bitcoins!

Receiving Tips From Customers

You don't need to be in the service industry to receive tips. If you have a blog, you can set up a Bitcoin payment gateway where your loyal fans and readers can tip you if they so desire.

Don't underestimate the generosity of your audience, especially if you produce content that provides a lot of value to them. Try it out – you just might be surprised to see some bitcoins in your wallet after a few days!

Complete Small Tasks On Websites

There are now plenty of sites on the Internet that offer free bitcoins (usually just a very, very small fraction of it) for every task you complete. Some websites require you to complete surveys, watch videos, click on ads, answer questions, sign up for trial offers, download mobile apps, play online games, refer friends, shop online, and more. Payment is usually quick and easy.

Some platforms just require your Bitcoin wallet address, while others require you to sign up and create an account. While it's true these jobs are mostly small and can be done in a few minutes, earning only a few hundred or thousand Satoshis at a time may not be worth it, especially if you value your time. But if you've got nothing better to do and you want to experience firsthand the joys of owning cryptocurrency, then you've got plenty of micro-tasking sites to choose from.

Join Bitcoin Faucets

Bitcoin faucets are just websites that give away free Satoshis at set time intervals. These sites bring in a huge amount of traffic from people wanting to get free bitcoins, so expect lots of competition and, depending on where the faucet is hosted, slow loading times.

Some faucets give away Satoshis with no work involved, meaning you just need to have the site open on your browser, while some require you to solve small tasks before you earn your Satoshis (much like the micro-tasking websites we've discussed in the previous section).

Sites like these can be a major time drain, so it's really up to you if you can afford to exchange your precious time for a few Satoshis.

However, we want to emphasize that Bitcoin mining isn't for everyone—and that's okay! While it's a fascinating process, it's best left to the experts or those with deep technical knowledge. The good news? There are plenty of other ways to get involved in the world of Bitcoin that don't require a huge investment of time or money.

As we've shown you in this guide, you can acquire Bitcoin through simple, accessible methods like buying on exchanges, earning through apps, or even participating in crypto rewards programs. The crypto world is full of opportunities, and you don't need to be a tech wizard to take advantage of them.

So, whether you're dipping your toes in or diving headfirst, remember: You've got this! The future of finance is here, and it's yours to explore. 💪✨

Women In Crypto

Here are some inspiring examples of women who have made significant contributions to the cryptocurrency and blockchain space:

1. Elizabeth Stark

- **Role:** Co-founder and CEO of Lightning Labs.
- **Contribution:** Elizabeth is a pioneer in blockchain scalability. Her work on the Lightning Network helps Bitcoin transactions become faster and cheaper, making it more practical for everyday use.

2. Cathie Wood

- **Role:** CEO of ARK Invest.
- **Contribution:** Cathie is a prominent investor who has been a strong advocate for Bitcoin and blockchain technology. Her investment firm, ARK Invest, has been a major supporter of crypto innovation.

3. Amber Baldet

- **Role:** Co-founder of Clovyr and former blockchain lead at JPMorgan.
- **Contribution:** Amber has been a key figure in bringing blockchain technology to mainstream finance. She now focuses on creating user-friendly decentralized apps (dApps) through her company, Clovyr.

4. Hester Peirce

- **Role:** Commissioner at the U.S. Securities and Exchange Commission (SEC).
- **Contribution:** Known as "Crypto Mom," Hester has been a vocal advocate for clear and fair regulations in the crypto space, helping to foster innovation while protecting investors.

5. Linda Xie

- **Role:** Co-founder of Scalar Capital and former product manager at Coinbase.

- **Contribution:** Linda is a well-respected investor and educator in the crypto space. She shares her knowledge through blogs and social media, helping newcomers understand blockchain technology.

6. Galia Benartzi

- **Role:** Co-founder of Bancor.
- **Contribution:** Galia is a leader in decentralized finance (DeFi). Bancor is a protocol that allows users to swap cryptocurrencies without needing a traditional exchange.

7. Laura Shin

- **Role:** Host of the Unchained Podcast and former senior editor at Forbes.
- **Contribution:** Laura is one of the most influential voices in crypto journalism. Her podcast and reporting help demystify blockchain technology for a broader audience.

8. Heather "Razzlekhan" Morgan

- **Role:** Entrepreneur and rapper (yes, really!).
- **Contribution:** Heather is a vocal advocate for crypto education and has used her unique platform to explain blockchain concepts in creative and accessible ways.

9. Perianne Boring

- **Role:** Founder and President of the Chamber of Digital Commerce.
- **Contribution:** Perianne is a leading advocate for blockchain adoption in the U.S. and works to promote pro-crypto policies and regulations.

10. Meltem Demirors

- **Role:** Chief Strategy Officer at CoinShares.
- **Contribution:** Meltem is a prominent figure in the crypto investment world and a strong advocate for women in tech and finance. She frequently speaks about the future of digital assets.

11. Me____________________(Add your name)

-Role:_____________________(What's your role in securing your future)

-Contribution______________________(How are you going to grow your generational wealth)

These women are breaking barriers and shaping the future of cryptocurrency and blockchain technology. Their work shows that crypto is not just a "boys' club" but a space where everyone can contribute and thrive!

What Is The Blockchain?

(Image Source: Biz2Credit)

Unlike normal currency transactions being confirmed and regulated through banks, cryptocurrency transactions are recorded on a public ledger known as the 'blockchain.'

Each block can be considered a page that contains transaction data. That is why it is called a blockchain. Mining helps to confirm these transactions on the blockchain.

Miners also run cryptographic hashes on blocks. A hash requires complex computations.

These hashes are important because they secure a block. Once a block has been accepted into the blockchain, it cannot be altered. Miners anonymously validate these transactions.

For their efforts, miners are rewarded with bitcoins. 'Proof of Work' is the term coined for the assistance of miners in validating transactions.

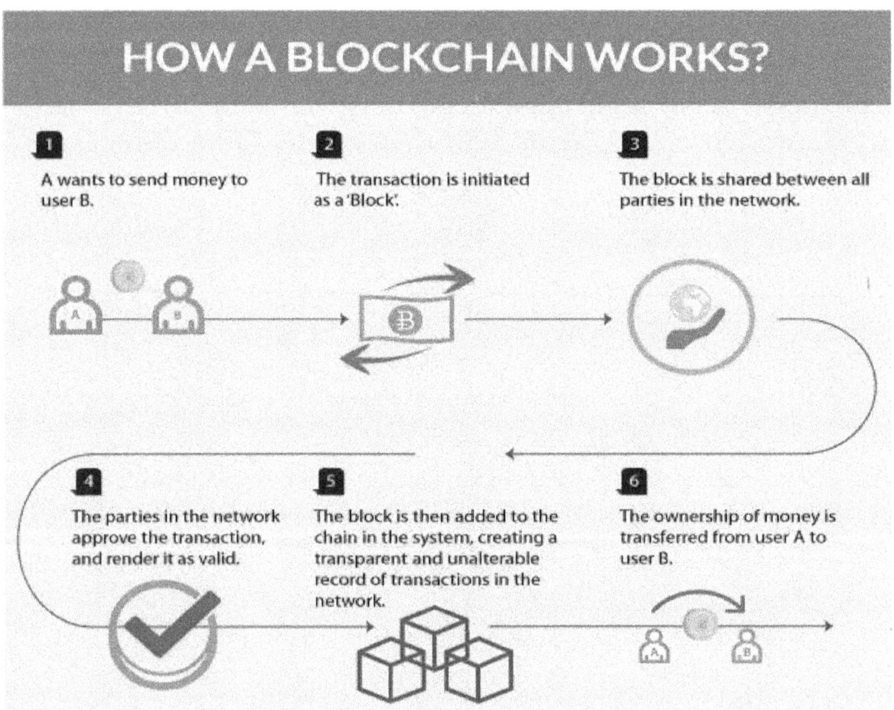

Trading And Selling Your Bitcoin For Profit

Trading and selling your Bitcoin can be a very profitable activity. You probably know someone or have heard about someone who bought bitcoins in the early days when they were worth almost nothing and ended up selling each Bitcoin for thousands of dollars!

Or you may know people who engage in trading bitcoins and are profiting very nicely as well. It might seem easy, but the truth is, trading bitcoins is not for everyone.

Beginners are especially advised to take caution and to be mentally and financially ready before taking the plunge into this exciting high-risk, high-reward world. When trading, it's common sense to follow the 'buy low and sell high' strategy to make a profit.

You don't want to sell at a price lower than when you bought in because you'll be selling at a loss. But all this sounds easy on paper.

In the real world, when you're dealing with bitcoins worth hundreds, thousands, or even millions of dollars, if you don't have the right mindset and financial discipline, you could panic very easily.

Especially if you're trading bitcoins that represent your entire life savings, your retirement fund, or your kids' college tuition!

Bitcoin Trading Strategies

Common sense and self-control should take precedence over greed and the idea of profiting thousands of dollars in a single day. Here are some Bitcoin trading strategies to guide you in the trading world.

Practice First

Learning the ins and outs of Bitcoin trading is great, but knowing just the theory is different from real-world application. Some Bitcoin exchanges offer a demo account where you can play around and experience real-world trading using real-time prices.

You'll get a feel for the landscape, so to speak, and you'll see for yourself whether you've got the stomach for the high-risk game of Bitcoin trading.

Plan Your Strategy

To trade bitcoins successfully, you need to have a good strategy in place. You don't just blindly follow the news and think that because everyone's buying bitcoins, then you should be buying too.

Have a plan in place on what price you should buy bitcoins at and what price to sell them to profit, and make sure you stick to that plan. This means keeping your panic at bay whenever you see the price drop.

Invest Small Amounts

As part of your practice or training strategy, you should start small and avoid going all in when you first trade. It is fine to lose all your 'money' in a demo account, but when it's real money, you don't want to risk losing huge sums on your first day.

Control Your Emotions

It's normal to feel alarmed at the first hint of losing your money. However, as you already know, Bitcoin is very volatile, and in a single day, the price can drop by hundreds or thousands of dollars. But the opposite is also true—the price can just as easily go up in the next hour or so.

If you keep your emotions in check and think logically, you too can make serious money with Bitcoin trading.

However, if you fail to control your emotions and let panic overcome you, then you're bound to lose.

Popular Bitcoin Trading Platforms

Now that you've learned some effective Bitcoin trading strategies, it's time to explore some of the most popular and trusted platforms for trading Bitcoin and other cryptocurrencies. These platforms cater to both beginners and advanced traders, offering user-friendly interfaces, robust security, and a wide range of features.

1. Coinbase

Overview:
Coinbase remains one of the largest and most trusted cryptocurrency exchanges globally, with over 110 million users across 100+ countries. Since its launch in 2012, Coinbase has facilitated over $1 trillion in trading volume.

Key Features:

- **Beginner-Friendly:** Simple interface for buying, selling, and storing cryptocurrencies.

- **Wide Range of Cryptos:** Supports Bitcoin (BTC), Ethereum (ETH), Litecoin (LTC), and 200+ other cryptocurrencies.
- **Security:** 98% of customer funds are stored offline in cold storage, and USD balances are FDIC-insured up to $250,000.
- **Coinbase Pro (Advanced Trading):** Offers lower fees and advanced trading tools for experienced users.
- **Mobile App:** Available for iOS and Android, making trading on the go easy.

How to Get Started:

1. Create a free account and verify your identity.
2. Link your bank account, debit card, or use Apple Pay/Google Pay for instant purchases.
3. Buy, sell, or trade cryptocurrencies directly on the platform.

Fees:

- Standard trading fees range from **0.5% to 4.5%**, depending on the payment method and transaction size.
- Coinbase Pro offers lower fees, starting at **0.4% for makers and 0.6% for takers**.

2. **Kraken**

Overview:
Kraken is a well-established cryptocurrency exchange founded in 2011, known for its high liquidity and strong security measures. It's particularly popular in Europe and supports a wide range of fiat currencies and cryptocurrencies.

Key Features:

- **Global Accessibility:** Supports trading in **USD, EUR, CAD, GBP, JPY,** and more.
- **Wide Crypto Selection:** Offers **200+ cryptocurrencies**, including Bitcoin, Ethereum, Solana (SOL), and Cardano (ADA).
- **Advanced Trading Tools:** Kraken Pro provides advanced charting, margin trading, and futures trading.
- **Security:** 95% of funds are stored in cold storage, and the platform has never been hacked.

How to Get Started:

1. Sign up for a free account and complete identity verification.
2. Deposit funds via bank transfer, wire transfer, or cryptocurrency.
3. Start trading on the user-friendly interface or use Kraken Pro for advanced features.

Fees:

- Trading fees start at **0.16% for makers and 0.26% for takers**, with discounts for higher trading volumes.

3. **Binance**

Overview:
Binance is the world's largest cryptocurrency exchange by trading volume, serving over **150 million users worldwide**. It offers an extensive range of cryptocurrencies and trading options.

Key Features:

- **Massive Crypto Selection:** Supports **350+ cryptocurrencies**, including Bitcoin, Ethereum, and emerging altcoins.
- **Low Fees:** Trading fees start at **0.1%** and can be reduced further using **Binance Coin (BNB)**.
- **Advanced Tools:** Binance offers **spot trading, futures trading, staking, and even NFT marketplaces**.
- **Binance Academy:** Free educational resources for beginners and advanced traders.

How to Get Started:

1. Create an account and complete **Know Your Customer (KYC)** verification (this process requires you to upload your ID, such as a driver's license or passport, and take a picture).
2. Deposit funds via bank transfer, credit card, or cryptocurrency.
3. Start trading on the platform or explore advanced features like **margin trading and staking**.

Fees:

- Standard trading fees are **0.1%**, with discounts available for using BNB or higher trading volumes.

4. Gemini

Overview:
Gemini is a U.S.-based cryptocurrency exchange founded by the Winklevoss twins. It's known for its strong regulatory compliance and user-friendly interface.

Key Features:

- **Security-First Approach: 95% of funds are stored in cold storage, and the platform is SOC 2-certified.**
- **Beginner-Friendly:** Simple interface for buying, selling, and storing cryptocurrencies.
- **Earn Program:** Allows users to earn interest on their crypto holdings.
- **Mobile App:** Available for iOS and Android.

How to Get Started:

1. Sign up and complete identity verification.
2. Link your bank account or debit card.
3. Start trading Bitcoin, Ethereum, and other supported cryptocurrencies.

Fees:

- Trading fees start at **0.5%** for active traders, with discounts for higher volumes.

5. Crypto.com

Overview:
Crypto.com is a popular platform offering a wide range of services, including **trading, staking, and a crypto-backed Visa card**.

Key Features:

- **Crypto Visa Card:** Earn cashback in cryptocurrency for everyday purchases.
- **Wide Crypto Selection:** Supports **250+ cryptocurrencies**.
- **Earn Program:** Earn interest on your crypto holdings with flexible and fixed-term options.
- **Mobile App:** Highly rated app for trading and managing your portfolio.

How to Get Started:

1. Create an account and complete **Know Your Customer (KYC)** verification (this process requires you to upload your ID, such as a driver's license or passport, and take a picture).
2. Deposit funds via bank transfer or credit card.
3. Start trading or explore additional features like **staking and the Visa card**.

Fees:

- Trading fees start at **0.4%**, with discounts for using Crypto.com's native token (**CRO**).

Why These Platforms Matter for Women

These platforms offer **accessibility, security, and educational resources**, making it easier than ever for women to dive into the world of cryptocurrency. Whether you're a beginner or an experienced trader, there's a platform tailored to your needs.

Final Thoughts

Choosing the right platform depends on your **goals, experience level, and preferred features**. Start small, explore your options, and remember: **The future of finance is in your hands. Let's make it count!** 🚀✨

Bitstamp

Founded in 2011 in the UK, Bitstamp is one of the pioneers in Bitcoin trading. They are constantly improving their services, and to date, they allow trading of Bitcoin, Ripple, Litecoin, Ether, and Bitcoin Cash. Bitstamp has a good reputation worldwide, especially since they accept trades from anyone in the world.

All major credit cards are accepted as well, making the platform very friendly to international users. They also promise no hidden fees with transparent volume-based pricing. Additionally, they guarantee that 98% of digital funds are stored offline for security.

Bitstamp does not sell bitcoins themselves. Instead, they provide a service or platform where people trade directly with each other—buyers get their bitcoins, and sellers get their cash at the price they want.

To get started with buying and selling bitcoins, you must create a Bitstamp account. You then need to transfer funds to your account via SEPA, wire transfer, or credit card. Once payment is credited, you can place an instant buy order, which will allow you to automatically buy bitcoins at the lowest price offered on the Bitstamp market.

A second option to buy bitcoins is by placing a limit order, where you can set the price you are willing to pay for bitcoins.

To sell bitcoins, you need to load your Bitstamp account with bitcoins first. Once you've done this, you can then place an instant sell order to automatically sell your bitcoins at the highest price offered on the market. Alternatively, you can place a sell limit order, where you can set the price at which you are willing to sell your bitcoins. Once your bitcoins are sold, you can proceed to withdraw your funds in USD or EUR currency.

Bitfinex

Since 2014, Hong Kong-based Bitfinex has been the world's largest cryptocurrency trading platform in terms of volume. This full-featured spot trading platform allows trades among major cryptocurrencies such as Bitcoin, Ethereum, Litecoin, Monero, Dash, Ripple, and more. Having such a large volume of Bitcoin exchanges happening on this platform implies the best liquidity.

This means you can trade a large volume of bitcoins at the price you want. Bitfinex's fees are also very low compared to other cryptocurrency exchanges, making it a preferred platform for traders who want to maximize their earnings instead of paying high transaction fees.

Funding your Bitfinex account is not as simple as with other exchanges. The only way to deposit money is via bank wire transfer, which can take several days. On top of the delay, Bitfinex charges a 0.1% fee on deposits, with a $20 minimum. Withdrawing your dollars is also a challenge, as the platform only offers bank wire withdrawals. Your funds may take up to 7 days to post to your account.

To avoid these inconveniences, trading experts suggest purchasing bitcoins or other cryptocurrencies elsewhere and then transferring them to your Bitfinex account. For withdrawals, you can transfer your crypto to a personal wallet and sell it locally. This workaround allows you to use Bitfinex strictly for trading cryptocurrencies.

Are You Ready to Start Trading Bitcoins?

There are many more Bitcoin and cryptocurrency exchanges that we haven't covered in this guide. It's essential to perform due diligence and research before selecting a trading platform. Just remember that whichever cryptocurrency exchange platform you choose, you must always move your cryptocurrency to a more secure wallet, such as a hardware wallet or paper wallet.

How to Store Your Crypto Safely

Once you're comfortable accumulating crypto on your preferred exchange, it's crucial to move your funds off the exchange and into a secure wallet. Leaving your crypto in an exchange wallet puts it at significant risk of being stolen by hackers. While exchanges have improved their security measures, they remain prime targets for cyberattacks.

1. Use a Hardware Wallet (Cold Storage)

What It Is: A hardware wallet is a physical device (like a USB drive) that stores your private keys offline, making it immune to online hacks.

Why It's Safe:

- **Offline Storage:** Your private keys never touch the internet, eliminating the risk of remote attacks.
- **Tamper-Proof:** Most hardware wallets are designed to resist physical tampering.

Popular Options:

- **Ledger Nano X/S:** Supports 1,800+ cryptocurrencies and offers Bluetooth connectivity.
- **Trezor Model T:** Features a touchscreen and supports 1,000+ cryptocurrencies.

How to Use:

1. Purchase a hardware wallet from the official manufacturer (avoid third-party sellers).
2. Set up the device and write down your **Recovery Seed Phrase** (store it securely offline).
3. Transfer your crypto from the exchange to your hardware wallet address.

2. Use a Software Wallet (Hot Wallet)

What It Is: A software wallet is an app or program that stores your private keys on your device.

Why It's Convenient:

- **Easy Access:** Ideal for frequent trading or small amounts of crypto.
- **User-Friendly:** Many software wallets are designed for beginners.

Popular Options:

- **Exodus:** Supports 250+ cryptocurrencies and has a built-in exchange feature.
- **Trust Wallet:** A mobile wallet that supports 4.5 million+ assets and integrates with decentralized apps (dApps).

How to Use:

1. Download the wallet app from the official website or app store.
2. Set up your wallet and securely store your **recovery phrase**.
3. Transfer your crypto from the exchange to your wallet address.

Important Note: Only keep small amounts of crypto in a hot wallet—enough for daily transactions or trading. Store the majority of your funds in a hardware wallet.

3. Use a Paper Wallet (For Advanced Users)

What It Is: A paper wallet is a physical printout of your **private and public keys**.

Why It's Safe:

- **Completely Offline:** No digital footprint, making it immune to hacking.
- **Low Cost:** Free to create if you have a printer and secure paper.

How to Use:

1. Use a trusted paper wallet generator (e.g., **BitAddress** or **WalletGenerator**).
2. Print your keys and store the paper in a secure location (e.g., a safe or safety deposit box).
3. Transfer your crypto to the paper wallet address.

Caution: Paper wallets are **less user-friendly** and can be **easily damaged or lost**. They're best for long-term storage of large amounts.

4. Use a Custodial Wallet (For Beginners)

What It Is: A custodial wallet is managed by a third party (e.g., an exchange or service provider).

Why It's Convenient:

- **Easy to Use:** No need to manage private keys.
- **Recovery Options:** If you lose access, the provider can help you recover your funds.

Why It's Risky:

- **Not Your Keys, Not Your Crypto:** You don't fully control your funds, and the provider could be hacked or go out of business.

Best Practice: Only use custodial wallets for small amounts of crypto you're actively trading or spending.

5. Follow Best Practices for Security

✓ **Backup Your Wallet:** Always write down your **recovery seed phrase** and store it in a secure, offline location (e.g., a fireproof safe).
✓ **Enable Two-Factor Authentication (2FA):** Use an authenticator app (e.g., **Google Authenticator**) for added security.
✓ **Beware of Phishing Scams:** Double-check URLs and **never share your private keys** or recovery phrase.
✓ **Diversify Storage:** Use a **combination** of hardware, software, and paper wallets to balance security and accessibility.

Final Thoughts

Storing your crypto securely is just as important as buying it. By moving your funds off exchanges and into secure wallets, you protect your investments from hackers and ensure you're in full control of your assets.

Remember: ***Not your keys, not your crypto.*** Take charge of your financial future by storing your crypto safely today! 🚀✨

Using Bitcoin As An Investment Strategy

Bitcoin is a relatively new form of currency that is just starting to gain traction and worldwide acceptance. With the recent exponential growth in the value of Bitcoin, many people are investing in this digital currency in hopes of reaping huge profits in the future.

In this guide, we will cover the basics of using Bitcoin as an investment strategy. Note that we are referring to long-term investment here, which is not the same as trading Bitcoin for short-term profits.

Investing in the highly volatile cryptocurrency market may not seem like a good idea for some people. Ideally, you'd need nerves of steel, the discipline and focus to ignore short-term gains, and the patience to hold your investment until the right time comes.

If you're truly determined to own a small share of the crypto market, then you should at least understand the most suitable methods so you can make the most of your investment.

Bitcoin Investment Methods

Dollar Cost Averaging Method

This strategy is best for beginners in the investing world because you don't need to worry about entering the market at the right time.

You don't have to stress yourself waiting for the price of Bitcoin to go down; instead, you buy at regular time intervals to spread the risk and hold/store your bitcoins in a cold, secure wallet (like a paper wallet or hardware wallet).

For example, if you have an extra $100 to spare every week, you can buy bitcoins every week. Some weeks your $100 may buy you more Bitcoin, and some weeks the same amount will buy you less.

This method gives you peace of mind because you don't need to worry about the dips in Bitcoin price.

You just have to be disciplined enough to follow your regular schedule and buy when you need to buy without looking at the Bitcoin price charts. You don't wait for the price to go down just because you see a downward trend on the charts—you simply stick to your buying schedule.

With the dollar cost averaging method, your profits will also average out when you decide to sell your bitcoins. It might not generate the same profits as the lump sum method, but if you sell at the right time (when the price is high), you'll still make a healthy profit from your investment.

Lump Sum Investing Method

The lump sum method is a much riskier way of investing in Bitcoin because you will be buying your bitcoins at a single price point.

If you have $100,000 to invest, you will, of course, want to buy the most bitcoins possible, so you wait for the price to go down. To maximize your investment, you will try to buy at the lowest possible price.

This method means you will have to 'time' the market to buy at just the right moment. Of course, this is easier said than done with a volatile asset like Bitcoin. The price fluctuates so much that it's extremely difficult to predict when the next price dip will occur.

Trying to time the market can cause a lot of stress for an inexperienced investor. It brings up too many 'what ifs,' such as:

- *"What if I wait a few more hours and the price drops, allowing me to buy more bitcoins?"*
- *"What if the price never goes down to my target, and I miss the opportunity to buy altogether?"*

When it comes to selling off your lump sum investment in the future, you may also struggle with timing the sale. You'll want to sell at the highest possible price, and you might regret selling too soon if the price keeps rising afterward.

The advantage of the lump sum investment method is that if you manage to buy at the lowest possible price and sell at the highest possible price, you will make a much bigger profit compared to the dollar cost averaging method. However, this requires significant patience, market knowledge, and risk tolerance.

Crypto Hedge Fund Investing Method

If you don't want to trouble yourself with learning the basics of investing using either the dollar cost averaging method or the lump sum method, you might be better off investing your money in a cryptocurrency hedge fund.

However, this option is best suited for people who can afford to pay hefty management and performance fees.

The management fee is paid upfront. Some funds require a 2% management fee, so if you're investing $100,000, $2,000 of that goes to the management fee, meaning only $98,000 is actually invested in cryptocurrency.

Additionally, your hedge fund manager will take a percentage of your profits. Some managers require a 20% performance fee, so if you profit $50,000 from your investment, $10,000 of that goes to the hedge fund manager.

The hedge fund method may not suit everyone, but if you look beyond the fees, it offers a hands-off approach to investing, which could prove to be highly profitable for both you and your hedge fund manager.

Strategies to Succeed in Bitcoin Investing

Investing in Bitcoin is similar to investing in stocks. Both are high-risk and high-reward investments, which, undoubtedly, are not for everyone.

Bitcoin is even more volatile than stocks, so if you want to invest in this cryptocurrency—or any other crypto, for that matter—you need to understand the following strategies to succeed.

Have a Solid Plan in Place

Don't invest blindly, and don't invest just because everyone you know has bought bitcoins. When investing, you need to have a solid plan in place, outlining your entry point and exit point.

Your plan should align with the investment method you choose. If you follow the dollar cost averaging method, establish a clear plan regarding how much and how often you'll be buying bitcoins.

For lump sum investing, determine in advance at what price you'll buy your bitcoins and stick to that price (don't wait for it to go any lower). For hedge fund investment, consider the fees involved and identify the best time to invest.

Be Prepared for Volatility

This is the number one strategy you need to master. Everyone knows that Bitcoin is a highly volatile investment, with prices fluctuating by hundreds of dollars in mere minutes. You might think you can handle the risk, especially if you've seen the charts, practiced on a demo Bitcoin exchange account, and read countless articles.

But when you have thousands of real dollars on the line, it's a different story—especially if you've worked hard to earn that money. The fear of losing months or years of savings in just a few minutes can be overwhelming.

The best approach is to ignore short-term dips. Instead of constantly checking the price, engage in other activities that help you stay relaxed. Bitcoin investing is like a roller coaster ride; you just need to hold on tight until you reach the end of the ride!

Keep Calm and Don't Panic

Telling others to stay calm is easy—but when you're the one panicking, it's a completely different experience. Watching thousands of dollars disappear in minutes can lead to irrational decisions.

If you don't think clearly, you might panic and sell your investment too soon, cutting your losses without considering long-term potential. If you play your cards right, your bitcoins could be worth significantly more than what you paid for them. But you'll never experience that growth if you panic and sell early.

Keep Perspective

Bitcoin investing is a long-term financial activity. It's different from day trading, which involves technical analysis to make quick profits. As a Bitcoin investor, you should zoom out and focus on the bigger picture.

Don't stress over daily, weekly, or even monthly price charts. Instead, look at Bitcoin's overall trajectory—from just a few cents in its early days to thousands of dollars now. Experts believe Bitcoin's upward trend will continue for years to come. If you ride out the highs and lows, you could build a valuable investment portfolio over time.

Don't Spend What You Can't Lose

This is one of the most important investment principles to remember. Cryptocurrency investing can make you insanely rich—or leave you bankrupt. However, you don't have to risk everything on Bitcoin.

The wisest approach is to only invest money you can afford to lose. That means not touching your emergency fund, retirement savings, or your kids' college tuition.

Many families have suffered financial ruin due to poor investment choices. If you've taken financial risks before and succeeded, don't assume you can replicate the same success with Bitcoin. The crypto market is unpredictable and still resembles the "Wild West" of investing.

Patience and Discipline Are Keys to Success

Bitcoin investing is a long-term game. You need patience when the price drops and discipline to hold onto your investment during market downturns.

If you study Bitcoin's history, you'll see that despite its volatility, it has generally followed an upward trend since its inception in 2009. The key is to ride out the lows and sell at the right peak when you're ready.

Bitcoin investing involves many ups and downs. You need the discipline to hold your investments when prices fall and the wisdom to avoid impulsively selling when prices rise too quickly. A solid plan, patience, and discipline are the keys to success.

Hindsight Is Always 20/20

Don't beat yourself up if you bought Bitcoin at a higher price than its current value. Likewise, don't regret selling too early if the price skyrockets after you've cashed out.

No one can predict the future. Instead of focusing on "what if" scenarios, aim to make a reasonable profit and stick to your strategy.

As the saying goes, hindsight is always 20/20. If everyone could see the future, we all would have invested in Bitcoin when Satoshi Nakamoto first introduced it.

Crypto Portfolio Recommendations

Here's a beginner-friendly crypto portfolio recommendation designed to balance risk, growth potential, and simplicity. This portfolio is ideal for someone just starting out in crypto and looking to build a solid foundation while minimizing exposure to high-risk assets.

1. Bitcoin (BTC) - 50%

Why Include It?

- Bitcoin is the gold standard of cryptocurrency, known for its scarcity, security, and store-of-value properties.
- It's the most established and widely adopted crypto, making it a relatively safe choice for beginners.

Role in Portfolio:

- Acts as the foundation of your portfolio, providing stability and long-term growth potential.

2. Ethereum (ETH) - 30%

Why Include It?

- Ethereum is the second-largest cryptocurrency and the leading platform for decentralized applications (dApps) and smart contracts.
- It's a key player in the growing sectors of DeFi (decentralized finance) and NFTs (non-fungible tokens).

Role in Portfolio:

- Adds growth potential through its utility and innovation in the blockchain space.

3. Stablecoins (e.g., USDC, USDT) - 10%

Why Include It?

- Stablecoins are pegged to fiat currencies like the US dollar, providing price stability.
- They're useful for holding value during market volatility or earning interest through staking or lending.

Role in Portfolio:

- Acts as a safety net, allowing you to quickly move funds during market downturns or take advantage of buying opportunities.

4. Altcoins (e.g., Solana, Cardano, Polygon) - 10%

Why Include It?

- Altcoins like Solana (SOL), Cardano (ADA), and Polygon (MATIC) offer high growth potential due to their innovative technologies and use cases.
- These projects focus on scalability, interoperability, and decentralized applications.

Role in Portfolio:

- Adds diversification and exposure to emerging trends in the crypto space.

Tips for Beginners

1. **Start Small:** Begin with an amount you're comfortable losing, as crypto markets can be volatile.
2. **Dollar-Cost Averaging (DCA):** Invest a fixed amount regularly (e.g., monthly) to reduce the impact of market fluctuations.
3. **Use Reputable Exchanges:** Platforms like Coinbase, Binance, or Kraken are beginner-friendly and secure.
4. **Secure Your Investments:** Move your crypto to a hardware wallet (e.g., Ledger or Trezor) for long-term storage.
5. **Stay Informed:** Follow trusted crypto news sources and communities to stay updated on market trends.

Why This Portfolio Works for Beginners

- **Balanced Risk:** The portfolio is weighted toward established assets (Bitcoin and Ethereum) while including a small allocation for higher-risk, higher-reward altcoins.
- **Simplicity:** It's easy to manage and understand, making it ideal for those new to crypto.
- **Growth Potential:** The inclusion of Ethereum and altcoins provides exposure to innovative projects and emerging trends.

Example Investment

If you're starting with $1,000, here's how your portfolio might look:

- **Bitcoin (BTC):** $500
- **Ethereum (ETH):** $300
- **Stablecoins (USDC/USDT):** $100
- **Altcoins (SOL, ADA, MATIC recommended; look within the top 100 Altcoins):** $100

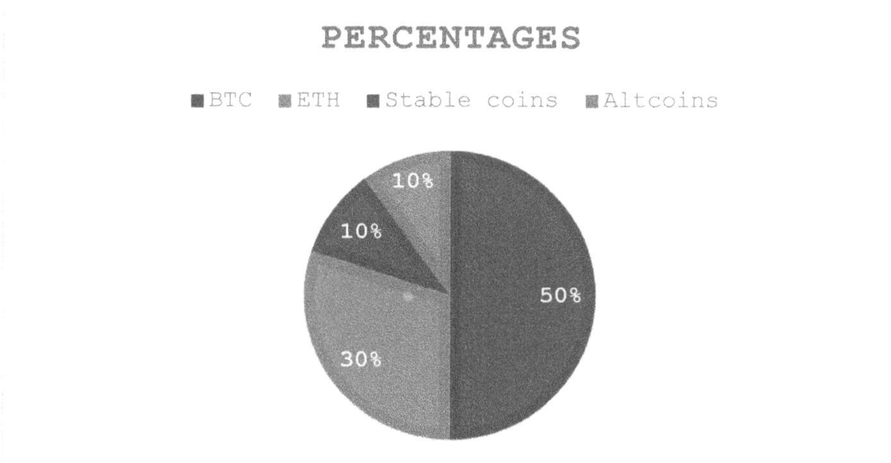

Here's a monthly Dollar-Cost Averaging (DCA) plan chart based on your example investment of $1,000, broken down into monthly contributions. This plan assumes you're investing $100 per month** and maintaining the same portfolio allocation:

Monthly DCA Plan Chart

Month	Bitcoin (BTC) 50%	Ethereum (ETH) 30%	Stablecoins 10%	Altcoins 10%	Total Monthly Investment
Jan	$50	$30	$10	$10	$100
Feb	$50	$30	$10	$10	$100
Mar	$50	$30	$10	$10	$100
Apr	$50	$30	$10	$10	$100
May	$50	$30	$10	$10	$100
Jun	$50	$30	$10	$10	$100
Jul	$50	$30	$10	$10	$100
Aug	$50	$30	$10	$10	$100
Sep	$50	$30	$10	$10	$100
Oct	$50	$30	$10	$10	$100
Nov	$50	$30	$10	$10	$100
Dec	$50	$30	$10	$10	$100

Total Annual Investment

Asset	Total Invested
Bitcoin (BTC)	$600
Ethereum (ETH)	$360
Stablecoins	$120

Altcoins	**$120**
Total	**$1,200**

Key Notes

1. Bitcoin (50%): $50 per month, totaling $600 annually.

2. Ethereum (30%): $30 per month, totaling $360 annually.

3. Stablecoins (10%): $10 per month, totaling $120 annually.

4. Altcoins (10%): $10 per month, totaling $120 annually.

Why This Plan Works

- Consistency: By investing $100 monthly, you reduce the impact of market volatility and avoid trying to time the market.

- Diversification: The portfolio is balanced between stable assets (Bitcoin, Ethereum) and growth opportunities (altcoins).

- Flexibility: You can adjust the amounts or allocations as you learn more about crypto or as your financial situation changes.

Example Altcoin Allocation

If you're investing $10 monthly in altcoins, here's how you might distribute it:

- **Solana (SOL):** $4

- **SUI (SUI):** $3

- **Uniswap (UNI):** $3

This DCA plan is a simple, disciplined approach to building your crypto portfolio over time.

Accepting and Using Bitcoin in Your Business

While many online and brick-and-mortar shops have added Bitcoin to their payment options, it's still not as widespread as the Bitcoin community would like it to be. Most business owners still prefer traditional payment methods simply because they don't know enough about Bitcoin or the benefits of adding it to their business.

Many don't trust Bitcoin due to its volatility. They fear that with such rapid fluctuations in the dollar-to-Bitcoin exchange rate, they could end up losing profits. This fear is understandable, but with today's innovations, this is no longer a major concern.

After all, many well-known companies like Microsoft, Overstock, Expedia, Wikipedia, WordPress.com, and Shopify are already accepting Bitcoin payments.

Online and Offline Businesses Can Accept Bitcoin Payments

Just because Bitcoin is a digital currency doesn't mean offline shops can't benefit from accepting Bitcoin payments.

- **For online shops**, you can integrate payment processors such as **Stripe, Coinbase, and Braintree** into your e-commerce checkout page.
- **For offline shops**, you can use Bitcoin terminals or **Point-of-Sale (POS) apps** like **XBTerminal, Coinify, or CoinGate**.
- You can also print out **QR codes** that customers can scan with their mobile wallets to easily pay in Bitcoin.

Once your Bitcoin wallet is set up, all you have to do is announce to the world that you're ready to accept Bitcoin payments!

How to Handle the Volatility of Bitcoin

The fear of losing profits due to Bitcoin's price volatility is a valid concern. However, with Bitcoin payment processors like Coinbase and BitPay, you can receive payments in Bitcoin and have them instantly converted into US dollars or another currency.

For example, if a customer pays you $100 worth of Bitcoin for a product, you will receive exactly $100 in your bank account. Your payment gateway, such as BitPay, shields you from Bitcoin's volatility so you always get the full amount.

For more experienced business owners willing to take the risk, holding onto Bitcoin instead of converting it to cash may offer an opportunity for even greater profits if Bitcoin's value rises.

Why Your Business Should Start Accepting Bitcoin Payments

Bitcoin was created by Satoshi Nakamoto in response to the 2008 financial crisis, which nearly crippled the global economy. It was designed to bypass the traditional banking system, which often benefits financial institutions more than consumers.

Consider the bank fees you pay every time someone makes a payment—deposit fees, withdrawal fees, transaction fees, credit card fees, and more. Bitcoin eliminates many of these unnecessary costs, allowing business owners to retain more of their hard-earned money.

The Benefits of Accepting Bitcoin Payments

1. No Risk of Chargebacks

Credit card and PayPal payments leave businesses vulnerable to chargebacks. Customers can dispute a charge for various reasons, including fraudulent claims, defective products, or even just to get something for free.

With Bitcoin payments, there is zero risk of chargebacks. Once a Bitcoin transaction is confirmed, it is final and cannot be reversed. No bank or government authority can undo the payment, offering merchants unparalleled protection.

2. No Fraud and Double Payments

Bitcoin is one of the most secure payment systems in existence. Unlike banks, Bitcoin is decentralized and incorruptible. Before Bitcoin, digital currencies were prone to fraud and double spending, but Nakamoto's blockchain technology solved this issue.

The Bitcoin network is transparent, with all transactions recorded on a public ledger called the blockchain. Transactions are only added to a block after being verified by miners, ensuring that they are legitimate. This system prevents double payments and fraudulent activities.

3. Near-Instant Payments

Bitcoin payments are fast, irreversible, and final. Once a customer sends Bitcoin to your address, the transaction is usually confirmed within 10-45 minutes.

However, ensuring that you provide the correct Bitcoin address is crucial. If you accidentally use the wrong address, there is no way to recover the lost funds—unless you personally know the recipient and can request a return.

For businesses using payment gateways like Coinbase or BitPay, cash withdrawals can take 2-3 days. These services process payments in batches and typically send out payments every business day.

Alternatively, if you prefer to hold Bitcoin rather than convert it to cash, you can select this option in your payment gateway settings. Whether you choose Bitcoin or fiat currency, you'll receive your funds faster and with fewer fees compared to PayPal or credit card transactions.

Negligible Transaction Fees

With Bitcoin payments, you get to keep more of what your customers pay you. By cutting out the middleman (your bank), you avoid expensive fees. While there is still a small Bitcoin transaction fee paid to miners who verify and record transactions on the blockchain, this fee is negligible—often just a few cents—compared to what banks or credit card companies charge.

For credit card payments, merchants typically pay an interchange fee (to the bank or card issuer) and an assessment fee (to Visa or Mastercard). These fees average around 3% to 4% per transaction.

In contrast, Bitcoin transaction fees are usually around 10,000 Satoshis (0.0001 BTC). You can set your own fee, but higher fees result in faster transaction confirmations by miners.

For example, a $1,000 credit card payment could cost a merchant $30 to $40 in fees. However, a Bitcoin transaction of the same amount would only cost about $1 if Bitcoin were priced at $10,000 per BTC.

Now, imagine selling a $1,000 product 10 times or 100 times a day—the savings on transaction fees alone could be substantial!

Increased Sales and More Profit for You

Bitcoin payments enable businesses to accept transactions from anywhere in the world. Traditional payment processors often block transactions from high-fraud regions, but Bitcoin has no such restrictions.

Platforms like PayPal and Stripe limit access in many countries, making it difficult for customers to complete purchases. With Bitcoin, all a customer needs is your Bitcoin address—no credit card details, ID verification, or lengthy approval processes.

Bitcoin's finality also eliminates the risk of chargebacks, allowing businesses to confidently accept payments without fear of fraud.

Happier Customers

Adding Bitcoin to your payment options provides an additional, convenient way for customers to pay. Even if they don't own Bitcoin yet, they may in the future, and they'll remember that your business accepts it.

If you're among the first businesses in your community to accept Bitcoin, you'll likely gain a reputation as an innovative and forward-thinking company. Customers who are curious about cryptocurrency may even look to you for guidance.

Wouldn't you rather be the business that attracts new customers through Bitcoin adoption, rather than losing them to a competitor that accepts it first?

Get Support from the Bitcoin Community

The Bitcoin community is growing rapidly, and as Bitcoin prices rise, holders are looking for places to spend their coins. While large corporations like Microsoft and Shopify accept Bitcoin, many businesses have yet to follow suit.

When Bitcoin users find a new business that accepts Bitcoin, they often share it on forums, social media, and crypto groups—giving you free publicity and new potential customers.

To maximize exposure, you can announce your Bitcoin acceptance on social media, join Bitcoin forums, and list your business on crypto directories. If you have a physical store, displaying a "Bitcoin Accepted Here" sign can also attract new customers.

Accepting Bitcoin isn't just about keeping up with trends—it's about growing your business, increasing sales, and maximizing profits.

How to Protect Yourself Against Fraud and Theft

Bitcoin and cryptocurrencies are hot commodities. With soaring prices, many people are eager to invest—but some resort to scams and theft instead.

In this guide, we'll highlight common crypto scams and how you can protect yourself.

A Costly Lesson: How I Lost $8,958 to a Crypto Scam

It all started with a message that seemed too good to be true—and it was.

I was browsing online when I stumbled across an ad promising 80% returns per day on my investment within just 2-3 days. The platform looked professional, complete with sleek charts and glowing testimonials. I thought, *Why not?* I had heard stories of people making life-changing money in crypto, and this seemed like my chance.

I invested $8,958—my hard-earned savings—into their "trading platform." For three days, I received notifications showing my investment growing rapidly. The charts looked real, the numbers were impressive, and I was thrilled.

But when I tried to withdraw my supposed $150,000 profit, the nightmare began.

First, they demanded exorbitant fees to "release" my funds. Then came the fake documents, the endless excuses, and the runaround. I realized too late that I had been scammed. The platform was a sham, the charts were fabricated, and my money was gone.

It was a painful lesson, but it taught me the importance of due diligence and skepticism in the crypto world.

Scam #1 – Fake Bitcoin Exchanges

There are plenty of reputable Bitcoin exchanges today. The biggest and most popular platforms that have been around for years include Coinbase, Kraken, CEX.io, Changelly, Bitstamp, Poloniex, and Bitfinex. However, even well-known exchanges should be approached with caution.

You must conduct thorough research, check user reviews, and verify the legitimacy of any exchange before entrusting them with your hard-earned money.

Too Good to Be True Exchange Rates

Due to the highly volatile nature of cryptocurrencies, many scammers exploit unsuspecting beginners who cannot differentiate between a legitimate exchange and a fake one.

These fake exchanges set up professional-looking websites and lure people in with promises of significantly lower-than-market prices and guaranteed returns. In essence, they prey on people's greed.

Imagine discovering a website offering Bitcoin at 10% or 20% below the rates on Coinbase or Kraken. If a well-known platform lists Bitcoin at $15,000 per BTC, but another site offers it at $12,000, wouldn't you be tempted?

Saving $3,000 per Bitcoin sounds like a fantastic deal—but that's exactly how scammers trap their victims. They know people want to buy more Bitcoin for less, and they exploit this desire.

Receive Instant PayPal Payment for Your Bitcoins

Another scam these fake exchanges use is promising to buy your Bitcoin at above-market rates and send the equivalent amount instantly to your PayPal account.

To the unsuspecting Bitcoin holder, this seems like an excellent deal—more money for their Bitcoin and instant cash in their PayPal account.

They enter the amount of Bitcoin they wish to sell, confirm the exchange rate, and provide their PayPal email. Then, they wait... and wait... and wait some more.

But the payment never arrives. When they try to contact the exchange, there's no response. By this point, the scammers have already stolen their Bitcoin (remember, Bitcoin transactions are final and irreversible).

Even if the victim writes bad reviews and reports the site, the scammers simply shut down and create a new website under a different domain name, waiting for their next victim.

The key takeaway here is simple: stay away from exchanges that offer rates that seem too good to be true. As the saying goes, if it's too good to be true, it probably is.

Scam #2 – Phishing Scams

Phishing scams come in many forms and are among the most common online threats. You may have encountered emails pretending to be from your bank, asking you to verify or update your account details by clicking a link.

Most people are aware that these emails are scams. Fortunately, modern email filters often flag them as junk mail. However, with Bitcoin and cryptocurrency gaining popularity, scammers have adapted their tactics to steal digital assets.

Email Phishing Scams

Scammers send emails that appear to be from legitimate crypto wallet services, attempting to trick users into revealing their login credentials.

These emails contain a link directing users to a fake website designed to look exactly like the real exchange or wallet service. However, a closer look reveals a slight difference in the domain name.

Common Fake Domains Used in Phishing Scams:

- Cooinbase (instead of Coinbase)
- Coiinbase
- Coinbasse
- Coinsbase
- Coinbase-Client-Update.com

Additionally, these fraudulent websites may lack SSL encryption, meaning the domain starts with "HTTP" instead of "HTTPS." Modern browsers like Chrome and Firefox usually warn users if a site is not secure.

If you fall for a phishing scam and enter your login details on the fake site, scammers immediately gain access to your real wallet. They can lock you out of your account and transfer every Bitcoin you own to their own wallets.

Malware Scams

In this type of scam, scammers will ask you to click on a link either via email, banner ad, forum ad, or anywhere they can post a link which will then download a type of malware to your computer.

Often, these malwares are keyloggers which will record everything you type on your computer and send the information to the scammers. So, if you log into your online wallet, like Coinbase for example, they will be able to see your username and your password, and they can then log in to your account and easily steal your coins from you!

The key takeaway for protecting yourself from these types of scams is to never click on links from untrustworthy sources.

If you don't recognize the sender, or the website's domain name is misspelled, it should raise a red flag, and you should report the email and/or leave the phishing site right away.

Furthermore, consider using offline storing methods such as paper wallets or hardware wallets so even if scammers get access to your online wallet, they'll have nothing to steal there.

Scam #3 – Cloud Mining Scams

Cloud mining is a popular way of becoming a bitcoin miner. You no longer need to invest in your own supercomputer and join a mining group to solve complex cryptographic hash problems. You don't even need to worry about expensive electricity bills.

You simply need to sign up to a cloud mining service (also known as a mining farm), rent mining equipment, and receive payments proportionate to your subscription.
While some cloud mining companies are legitimate, there are many fly-by-night websites which promise unrealistic returns for measly sums, whose sole purpose is to steal your money.

Some common red flags to watch out for when looking to join a cloud mining service is the absence of an About page, Terms of Use/Service page, physical address, and/or contact number.

They might also not have a secure domain (no HTTPS before their domain name). These details are all very important in figuring out which site is a scam and which is not. You can search Google for reviews and go through their website to get a feel if they're legitimate or not. More often than not, these sites would be anonymous with no names or faces behind them.

Some may appear legitimate at first but take a deeper look at what your investment's going to get you. You may pay eventually and sign up for a contract which is going to cost you a few thousand dollars a year but what are you going to get in return? You'll have to do the math yourself and calculate if you're going to end up in the green.

The key takeaway here is before you spend any of your hard-earned fiat money, you should at least make sure you're dealing with a legitimate company and not some anonymous scammer who'll leave you in tears. Do plenty of research, read reviews, and browse the crypto mining communities for information on the best and most trustworthy cloud mining companies.

Scam #4 – Ponzi Scams

Ponzi scams are probably easier to spot than the other scams we've covered so far in this guide. This is because Ponzi scams are well known for guaranteeing outlandish returns on investments with little to no risk to the investors. People fall for these sorts of scams all the time because people want guaranteed returns on their investments.

With Bitcoin and cryptocurrency, any company that guarantees exponential returns on any investment should be viewed as a potential scammer. The cryptocurrency market is highly volatile, and one minute the price could be at an all-time high and the next, it's down by a few hundred or a few thousand dollars.
Because of this volatility, you should never believe anyone who tells you you're guaranteed a 10% return on your investment every single day, or whatever the scammer's terms may be.

Since Ponzi schemes rely on new members, a.k.a. victims, to pay off their early investors, they usually offer incentives for members to recruit new people to join their network.

It's very common for scams like this to offer some form of affiliate rewards. You refer someone to invest in the 'company,' and you get compensated for your efforts.

Some Ponzi schemes guarantee daily profits forever. If this seems impossible, it most certainly is. No one even knows if bitcoins will be around that long and guaranteeing daily returns is just crazy. Right off the bat, an intelligent investor will see that offers like these are nothing more than scams designed to rip you off your money or your bitcoins.

In fact, many of these scam sites prefer bitcoin payments because they know Bitcoin transactions can't be reversed or canceled once sent! Either way, whether they require fiat or cryptocurrency, know who you're sending your money to first.

The key takeaway here is if you know the company's offers are too good to be true, then you should run away in the opposite direction. Sometimes, there's just no point in even looking up reviews on the Internet when it comes to scams like these because most 'reviewers' are those who got in the game early and thus have already received some return on their investment. And usually, when these users leave reviews, they'll include their affiliate link so you know right away they have a vested interest for leaving glowing reviews for a company they may, or may not know, is a scam.

How to Protect Yourself Against Fraud and Theft

1. **Avoid "Get Rich Quick" Schemes:** If it sounds too good to be true, it probably is. Legitimate investments don't promise astronomical returns in days.

2. **Research Platforms:** Only use reputable exchanges and wallets. Check reviews, verify licenses, and look for red flags.

3. **Never Share Private Keys:** Your private keys are like the keys to your bank vault—never share them with anyone.

4. **Beware of Phishing Scams:** Double-check URLs and avoid clicking on suspicious links or emails.

5. **Use Two-Factor Authentication (2FA):** Add an extra layer of security to your accounts.

6. **Trust Your Instincts:** If something feels off, walk away.

Final Thought

Crypto is an exciting space, but it's also a playground for scammers. By staying informed and vigilant, you can protect yourself and your investments. Remember: If it seems too good to be true, it probably is. Even those expensive video commercials raving about the person who has been in the field of investments for over 100 years lol, but seriously, please protect yourself and your family's general wealth.

Let my story be a cautionary tale—don't let greed cloud your judgment. Stay safe, and happy investing! 🚀✨

Bitcoin and Cryptocurrencies Are Not Scams

Before we go into the main scams you should be aware of, we'd like to point out that these scams are all from outside forces, and not cryptocurrencies themselves. You might hear some people say that cryptocurrencies are nothing but a huge scam, but it's 100% false, and we'll explain why.

The technology behind cryptocurrencies is called the blockchain. It is an incorruptible digital ledger that records all transactions on the network. No central body controls it. It is transparent, and anyone can track any transaction that has ever happened in the past.

No one can alter any transaction recorded on the blockchain because doing so would mean you'd have to alter the rest of the transactions or blocks that came after that particular transaction; this is virtually an impossible task to do.

The blockchain is so secure that many banks and startup companies are now experimenting and starting to implement blockchain technology because they've seen just how well it works on Bitcoin and cryptocurrencies.

Now that you know you can trust the technology behind cryptocurrencies, let's discuss the most common scams that many people fall prey to.

The Future of Cryptocurrency

Before we talk about the future of cryptocurrency, it's important to remind ourselves of the past and what cryptocurrency was like in the beginning.

Back in 2008, when Bitcoin founder Satoshi Nakamoto first released his whitepaper on Bitcoin, many people said it was just a fad and a scam designed to trick people into giving up their 'real' money.

There were many naysayers and financial experts who said Bitcoin would never be adopted by the masses and would fizzle out in a year or so.

Fortunately, the cryptocurrency community rallied and worked together to make Bitcoin a success. They saw potential in blockchain technology and what it could mean for the finance sector. They saw the need for cryptocurrency because the current financial setup via banks and governments had too many problems and was causing national economies to collapse.

They saw that keeping inflation at bay was difficult with traditional currencies and that the poorest people often had no easy access to banks. Receiving or sending payments was oftentimes a headache, with transaction fees eating up a significant amount of money.

Banks charge exorbitant fees just so their customers can get access to their own money, and the government takes very little action, if at all, to help the people.

Bitcoin supporters say the modern financial system is a mess where banks and governments collude or work together—not to help their citizens' financial needs, but to take as much money as they can from them in terms of fees collected.

Bitcoin changed all that. With Bitcoin, you're cutting out the middleman. There are no more banks to deal with and no government to spy on your bank accounts. With Bitcoin, you are your own bank. You're the bank teller sending and receiving payments, and you're the banker in charge of keeping your money safe.

Bitcoin has been a leader on so many fronts. As the first successful cryptocurrency, it has paved the way for other cryptocurrencies to succeed, and the global community has slowly taken notice over the past few years.

Read on to find out what other possibilities Bitcoin and cryptocurrencies bring for the future!

Massive Support From The Masses

In most developed countries, getting a credit card or a business loan is relatively easy. However, in developing countries, you'd have to literally jump through hoops and government red tape before you can get one. But with Bitcoin and cryptocurrency, all you need is just your digital wallet, and you can start receiving cryptocurrency from anyone, anywhere in the world. You don't even need your own Internet connection at home; you can simply go somewhere with good Internet access and create a quick wallet online or on your mobile phone. Of course, storing your crypto online is not a good idea, so you should look into storing these in cold storage, such as a hardware wallet or paper wallet.

But online wallets are great for small transactions, so if you need to pay a utility bill or your credit card bill, simply scan the utility company's Bitcoin wallet's QR code and send your crypto payment. No need to spend the whole day standing in long lines!

Today, there are already many businesses that have started to accept Bitcoin payments (though they are still in the minority). These forward-thinking business owners see the benefit of accepting Bitcoins and are profiting nicely from this smart business decision!

You can buy virtually anything with Bitcoins. You can buy plane tickets, rent cars, pay for your college tuition, buy groceries, purchase items on Amazon by getting Amazon gift cards from third-party sites, and so much more!

In the future, we can expect many more businesses to jump onto the Bitcoin payment wagon, which would be a win-win situation for both business owners and customers. Businesses will receive their payment fast and into their bank accounts the very next day (using a payment gateway like BitPay, which offers instant Bitcoin-to-fiat currency conversion), and customers will be able to buy items in a very convenient manner.

Bitcoin In Developing Economies

It's not surprising that Bitcoin has seen massive adoption in recent years. In fact, in Zimbabwe, people are using Bitcoins to make financial transactions. With the demise of the Zimbabwean dollar, the country had to resort to using US dollars as their main currency.

However, this is not a very feasible solution because their government can't print US dollars themselves. Venezuelans are also experiencing the same problem. The Venezuelan bolivar has become so hyper-inflated that it's almost unusable. People have resorted to using Bitcoins to pay for basic goods, medicines, groceries, and much more.

For Zimbabweans, Venezuelans, and citizens of countries with super-inflated currencies, Bitcoin is a beacon of light because it's not subject to the whims and manipulations of their local banks or governments.

Their present economic situation is a perfect example of the downside of having a central authority manage a country's currency, while at the same time, it highlights all the benefits of using Bitcoin—a decentralized and 100% transparent financial network.

With Bitcoin getting massive support from people in developing countries, governments may soon step in to regulate the use of Bitcoin and other cryptocurrencies. While we can't predict the future, for now, Bitcoin provides a wonderful inflation-resistant alternative to traditional currency.

And with skyrocketing Bitcoin and cryptocurrency prices, this gives many people greater purchasing power that their national currencies cannot provide.

Fast And Cheap International Payments

One of the main benefits of Bitcoin payments is the speed by which the recipient can receive their Bitcoins. This is perfect for people who hire freelancers or employees overseas.

The employees don't need to sign up for a bank account and incur fees left and right just because they're receiving money from an international client.

Of course, we must also mention the fees that the sender pays to their bank every time they remit or transfer money to overseas workers.

In addition to the fees both sender and recipient pay, you'd also have to factor in the exchange rate. Most banks and money transfer services will usually advertise an exchange rate, but when compared to actual rates, the bank rate is much lower.

Even for PayPal payments, the exchange rate they use tends to be different. You might not notice the difference when transferring small amounts, but when transacting in thousands of dollars, the fees quickly add up to a significant amount.

With Bitcoin, you can say goodbye to all these exorbitant fees.

For every Bitcoin transaction, you do need to pay a small fee for the miners, but it's literally nothing compared to what banks charge!

Whether you're sending 1,000 Bitcoins or 0.01 Bitcoins, the mining fee can be the same since fees are computed in terms of bytes, not the amount of Bitcoin transacted.

The size (in bytes) of a transaction depends on the number of inputs and outputs per transaction. Without going into technical details, the key takeaway here is that mining fees are very small compared to bank fees.

This is why Bitcoin and cryptocurrency are going to change the future. More people will transact with each other directly to avoid paying excessive bank fees!

With more and more people sending cryptocurrency to each other directly, third-party money transfer services or even banks may eventually become obsolete. Though this may take many years, it's still a possibility once the benefits of using cryptocurrency become widely understood.

Combat Crime and Corruption

Many people worry that the Bitcoin network is being used by money launderers, criminals, and corrupt officials because they think it's an anonymous network. While all verified transactions are recorded on the blockchain, no names are listed—only alphanumeric codes.

If you download the free and open-source Bitcoin Core client, you'll need to download the entire blockchain, which is already over 100GB in size. Millions of Bitcoin transactions since 2009 are stored on the blockchain, including the first-ever transaction by Bitcoin's founder, Satoshi Nakamoto.

We're mentioning this to highlight that Bitcoin is not truly anonymous. Instead, it is pseudonymous, meaning users can hide behind pseudonyms, but upon close inspection, digital forensics experts can trace Bitcoin wallet ownership.

This process can be time-consuming, but when criminals launder millions or billions of dollars' worth of Bitcoins, catching them becomes a top priority. In fact, experts say that criminals are better off stashing their stolen funds in offshore bank accounts, where strict bank privacy laws make tracking more difficult.

However, Bitcoin is easier to move around, so some believe they can hide illicit transactions in the blockchain's alphanumeric maze.

The reality is that Bitcoin's transparency has actually helped law enforcement track and catch criminals. Several high-profile cybercriminals and money launderers have been caught thanks to blockchain analysis.

In the future, if and when cryptocurrency gains massive support and adoption worldwide, it will become even easier for authorities to trace and catch criminals hoping to use cryptocurrencies to hide and move stolen money.

Blockchain Technology Will Become Mainstream

Many governments, banks, and private organizations are looking into adopting blockchain technology into their products and services. The blockchain is the underlying technology behind Bitcoin and other cryptocurrencies. Technology is already starting to receive recognition and adoption from many sectors in the world. While this may take several years, it's at least a positive nod in favor of the blockchain revolution.

Two of the most popular blockchain technologies today are Ethereum and Hyperledger. You may have heard of Ethereum as the second most popular cryptocurrency, after Bitcoin. But it's more than just a virtual currency platform. Ethereum is a platform that allows anyone to create smart contracts which help people trade or exchange anything of value, such as money, property, stocks, etc. The contract is publicly transparent and is recorded on the blockchain, which means other people are witnesses to the agreement.

The best thing about smart contracts is that you are basically automating contracts without paying for the services of a middleman such as a bank, stockbroker, or lawyer. Hyperledger, on the other hand, is an open-source, cross-industry collaborative project with contributors from many major companies such as Deutsche Bank, IBM, Airbus, and SAP. According to their website, the collaboration aims to develop a "new generation of transactional applications that establish trust, accountability, and transparency." These applications have the potential to streamline business processes and reduce the cost and complexity of various systems in the real world.

These are just a few examples of how blockchain technology is going to change the world in the future. Blockchain may be less than a decade old, but it has already changed the lives of so many people for the better.

Will You Be A Part Of The Cryptocurrency Revolution?

In this guide, you've learned so many benefits of using Bitcoin, cryptocurrency, and blockchain technology. Investing in cryptocurrency may be in your best interest, though it's always best to do in-depth research on which cryptocurrency to invest in. Bitcoin may be too expensive for now, but remember that you don't have to buy a whole Bitcoin. Alternatively, there are other emerging cryptocurrencies with good track records you may consider investing in. With cryptocurrency looking set to get integrated with mainstream financial markets, investing in cryptocurrency is not a scary thought anymore. In fact, it just might be the best financial decision you'll ever make for yourself and your family's future.

The Future of Women in Cryptocurrency Investing

The landscape of cryptocurrency investing is evolving, and women are increasingly finding their place within this dynamic sphere. As more women become aware of the potential opportunities in cryptocurrency, they are positioning themselves not just as participants but as leaders and innovators. The future of women in cryptocurrency investing is promising, with a growing network of resources and communities that support female entrepreneurs and investors. This shift is fostering an environment where women can confidently engage with cryptocurrency, develop their investment strategies, and navigate the intricacies of blockchain technology.

One of the key factors influencing the future of women in cryptocurrency is the increasing availability of educational resources tailored specifically for female investors. These resources often address the unique challenges women face in the financial world, such as societal biases and lack of representation. By providing targeted education on cryptocurrency investment strategies, platforms are empowering women to make informed decisions. This includes understanding market trends, recognizing investment opportunities, and effectively managing risks associated with volatile assets.

Risk management is another critical component of cryptocurrency investing that women are beginning to master. As they dive into the world of digital currencies, female investors can adopt strategies that are suited to their personal financial goals and risk tolerance levels. Understanding the importance of diversification, setting stop-loss orders, and conducting thorough due diligence are essential skills that can help mitigate the inherent risks of cryptocurrency investment. By building a solid foundation in risk management, women can approach cryptocurrency investing with confidence and resilience.

Blockchain technology, the backbone of cryptocurrencies, also presents unique opportunities for women. Understanding this technology from a women's perspective can unlock new avenues for innovation and entrepreneurship. Women can leverage their insights to create solutions that address gaps in the market, such as applications focused on social impact or improved accessibility. By participating in blockchain development and advocacy, women can shape the future of this technology and enhance its potential to foster economic empowerment.

Lastly, tailored cryptocurrency portfolio management is essential for women looking to build wealth through digital assets. Female investors often prioritize values-based investing, seeking to align their portfolios with their personal beliefs and long-term objectives. This approach not only enhances investment outcomes but also contributes to the broader goal of creating a more equitable financial landscape. By developing strategies that consider their unique perspectives and aspirations, women can cultivate a cryptocurrency portfolio that reflects their individual identities and ambitions, paving the way for a more inclusive future in the world of finance.

BONUS

Creating a simple crypto ledger to track your transactions is an excellent way to manage your cryptocurrencies effectively. You can use a spreadsheet application like Microsoft Excel, Google Sheets, or another simple database format to create your ledger. Below is a template structure you can use in a spreadsheet to track your cryptocurrency transactions.

Cryptocurrency Transaction Ledger Template

You can set up your ledger with the following columns:

Date	Transaction Type	Cryptocurrency	Amount	Price per Coin	Total Value	Wallet/Exchange	Notes
YYYY-MM-DD	Buy/Sell/Transfer	BTC/ETH/LTC/ADA	0.5	$35,000	$17,500	Binance	Buy for investment
YYYY-MM-DD	Buy/Sell/Transfer	BTC/ETH/LTC/ADA	1.0	$30,000	$30,000	Coinbase	Sold to realize gains
YYYY-MM-DD	Buy/Sell/Transfer	BTC/ETH/LTC/ADA	0.2	$40,000	$8,000	Personal Wallet	Gift to a friend
YYYY-MM-DD	Buy/Sell/Transfer	BTC/ETH/LTC/ADA	0.1	$39,500	$3,950	Kraken	Staking rewards
YYYY-MM-DD	Buy/Sell/Transfer	BTC/ETH/LTC/ADA	0.25	$38,000	$9,500	Binance	Bought more

Explanation of Each Column:

Transaction Ledger Fields

1. **Date:** The date when the transaction took place.
2. **Transaction Type:** Specify whether the transaction was a "Buy," "Sell," or "Transfer."
3. **Cryptocurrency:** The type of cryptocurrency you are dealing with (e.g., Bitcoin, Ethereum, Litecoin).
4. **Amount:** The quantity of cryptocurrency involved in the transaction.
5. **Price per Coin:** The price of the cryptocurrency at the time of the transaction.

6. **Total Value:** This is calculated by multiplying the amount of cryptocurrency by the price per coin (**Amount × Price per Coin**).
7. **Wallet/Exchange:** Indicate where the transaction took place (e.g., exchange platforms like Binance, Coinbase, or personal wallets).
8. **Notes:** Include any relevant details about the transaction (e.g., reason for the purchase or sale, transaction ID).

Steps to Create Your Ledger

1. **Choose Your Tool:** Use Microsoft Excel, Google Sheets, or another spreadsheet application.
2. **Set Up Columns:** Create a spreadsheet with the above column headers.
3. **Entering Data:** Log each transaction immediately after it occurs, including all relevant details.
4. **Use Formulas:** Utilize formulas for calculating the **Total Value** automatically in the spreadsheet.
    - For example, in Excel or Google Sheets, you can use the formula for the **Total Value** column like this: =C2*D2 (assuming **Amount** is in column C and **Price per Coin** is in column D).
5. **Review Regularly:** Regularly review your ledger to track performance and manage your portfolio effectively.

Additional Tips:

- **Backup:** Regularly back up your data to ensure you don't lose any important records.
- **Categorize Transactions:** You may want to create additional categories based on the purpose of each transaction (e.g., investment, trading, gifts) for better tracking.
- **Consider Security:** If you're using spreadsheets for sensitive information, ensure that your files are secure and encrypted as needed.

This simple crypto ledger will help you effectively track your cryptocurrency transactions and provide insights into your investments over time.

Promise Agreement to Myself

I, [Your Name], hereby make a commitment to take control of my financial future by embracing the opportunities presented by cryptocurrency. Recognizing its potential to revolutionize the global financial system, I promise to:

1. **Educate Myself:** I will take the time to learn about blockchain technology, cryptocurrencies, and how they work.
2. **Invest Wisely:** I will start small, diversify my portfolio, and avoid impulsive decisions driven by fear or greed.
3. **Stay Informed:** I will keep up with market trends, news, and developments in the crypto space.
4. **Protect My Investments:** I will prioritize security by using reputable platforms, enabling two-factor authentication (2FA), and storing my crypto in secure wallets.
5. **Think Long-Term:** I will focus on building wealth over time rather than chasing quick profits.
6. **Share Knowledge:** I will help my family and loved ones understand the potential of cryptocurrency and how it can benefit our future.

I believe that investing in cryptocurrency is not just a financial decision but a step toward financial freedom and empowerment. By staying disciplined, informed, and proactive, I am confident that this journey will lead to a brighter future for myself and my family.

Signed:

____

[Your Name]

Date: ______________________

This promise agreement is a personal commitment to take charge of your financial future through cryptocurrency. 🚀✨

Resources Section

- Books: "The Bitcoin Standard" by Saifedean Ammous.
- Websites: CoinMarketCap, CoinGecko, and Bitcoin.org.
- YouTube Channels: Andreas Antonopoulos, Coin Bureau.
- Podcasts: "The Pomp Podcast" by Anthony Pompliano.

Savvy Publisher

456 Oceanview Drive
San Diego, CA 92101

www.ingramcontent.com/pod-product-compliance
Lightning Source LLC
LaVergne TN
LVHW050938210926
848482LV00013B/662